For Deborah & Michael

A preview of the beautiful art I will see this Winter — This book is the production of the gallery owners where I "babysit" a few times a week

Thought you would enjoy for your library

Merry Christmas

2004

Marc

Treasures of Chinese Glass Work Shops

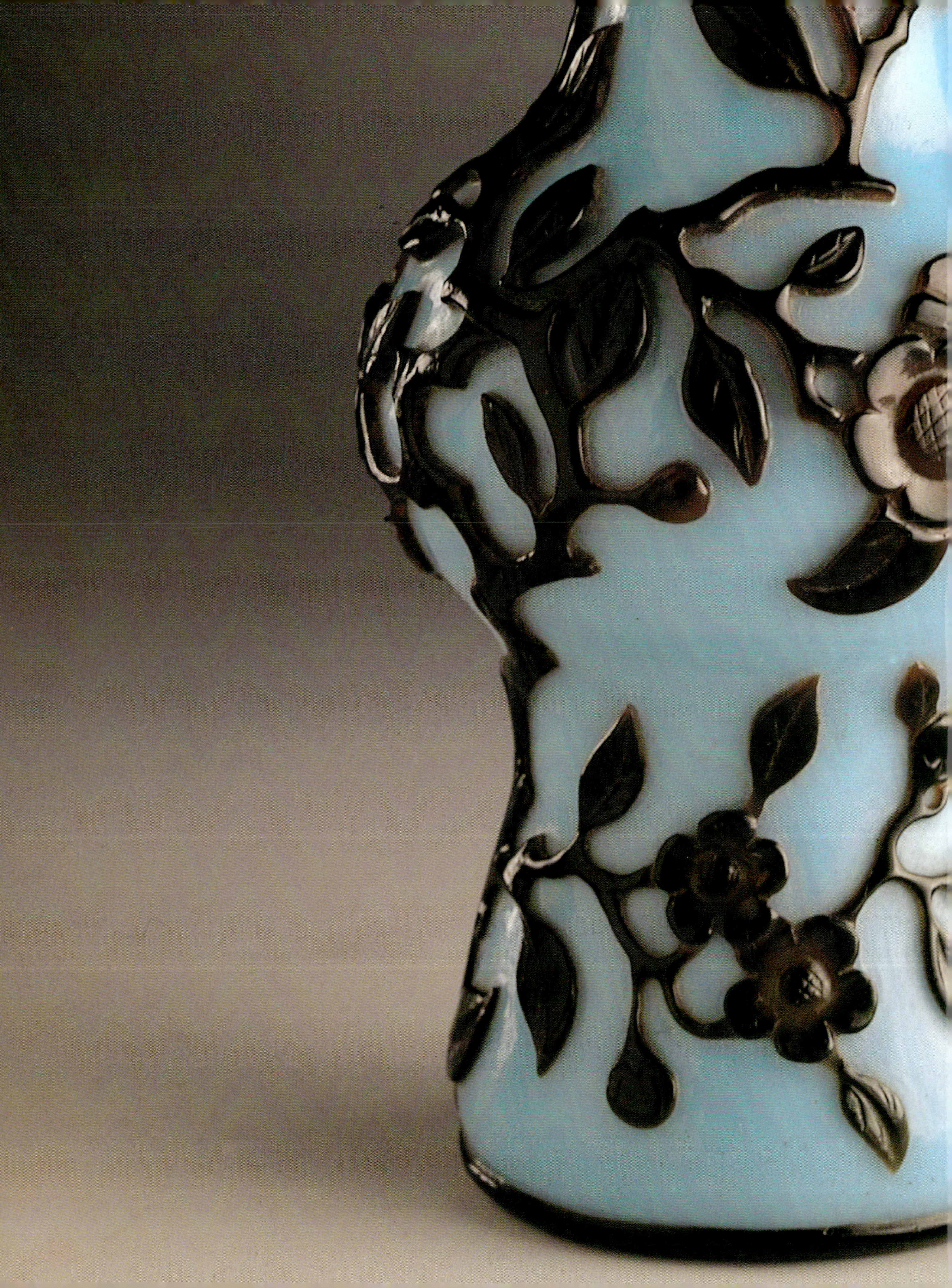

Treasures of Chinese Glass Work Shops

Selection of Chinese Qing Dynasty Glass in the Ina and Sandford Gadient Collection

presented by

Asiantiques

Published by Asiantiques, Inc. 130 North Park Avenue Winter Park, FL 32789
Distributed by Art Media Resources, Ltd.

Production supervision for Asiantiques, Inc. by Philippe Lorin
Photography by Martinot Photo Studio, Inc (407) 688-8746
Design by Anne Chaponnay
Printed and bound in the European Community

Jacket and cover: Vase of pear shape, page 52
Back cover: vase, page 70
Frontispiece: vase of gu-shape (detail), page 71
Page 15: vase of hu shape, page 22

ISBN 1-875529-24-2

Asiantiques, Inc, 130 North Park Avenue, Winter Park, FL 32789
(407) 629 - 9118 ■ Fax (407) 629 - 0818 ■ www.asiantiques.com
Art Media Resources, Ltd. 1507 South Michigan Avenue Chicago, IL 60605
(312) 663-53-51. Fax (312) 663-5177

Contents

ORLANDO MUSEUM OF ART

2416 North Mills Avenue

Orlando, Florida 32803-1483

407/896-4231

April 15, 1997

Mr. and Mrs. Francois Lorin
Asiantiques
130 Park Avenue
Winter Park, Florida 32789

Dear Mr. and Mrs. Lorin:

It is wonderful to see the entire Central Florida community supporting the *Imperial Tombs of China* exhibition coming to Orlando Museum of Art May 2-September 15, 1997.

This community wide tribute to Asian art and culture should create a better understanding of the accomplishments of these ancient civilizations. We are very grateful to you for the contributions you have made through your lectures and your current exhibition. We are fortunate to have expertise such as yours in our community.

Warm regards,

Marena

Marena Grant Morrisey
Executive Director

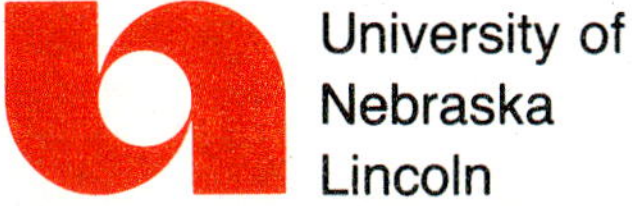

Lentz Center for Asian Culture
329 Morrill Hall
14th and U Street
P.O. Box 880372
Lincoln, NE 68588-0372
(402) 472-5841

April 29, 1997

It is my great pleasure to congratulate the Gadients on this new and expanded exhibition of their Chinese glass collection. The Lentz Center for Asian Culture at the University of Nebraska was privileged to present their first exhibition, *Bounties of the Qing: Selections from the Hilmes and Gadient Collections* for which the Gadients joined with their old friends and fellow Chinese glass lovers, Phil and Margaret Hilmes.

The Lentz Center exhibition (October 21, 1994-January 14, 1995) was not only a first for me as the new Director/Curator, but was also a first for the Center and for the State. Very well received by the public and the press, it served as a bridge between collector, curator, and the art community. It provided greater understanding of the dynamic nature of Qing Dynasty glass objects. The uncompromisingly vivid colors, the variety of surface decor, and the varying levels of translucency made the Chinese glass a memorable visual experience, as well as a public learning opportunity.

The residents and visitors in Florida are indeed fortunate to have the opportunity to view this private collection at the Asiantiques Gallery in Winter Park this summer, held concurrently with the exciting travelling exhibition, *Imperial Tombs of China,* at the Orlando Art Museum. As the *Imperial Tombs of China* contains many Qing Dynasty artifacts, the timing is especially fortuitous.

Without the generosity of collectors like Sandford, Ina, and Elizabeth Gadient, our knowledge of arts such as Chinese glass would be severely limited. Please accept my best wishes for success in your forthcoming exhibition entitled *Treasures from Chinese Glass Workshops: Selections of Qing Dynasty Glass in the Ina and Sandford Gadient Collection.*

Barbara Chapman Banks

Barbara Chapman Banks, Ph.D.
Director/Curator
Lentz Center for Asian Culture

University of Nebraska–Lincoln University of Nebraska Medical Center University of Nebraska at Omaha University of Nebraska at Kearney

Preface

The exquisite beauty of Chinese Glass has fascinated us for over 25 years, since the collection started while residing in Hawaii in the early 1970's, during which time frequent trips were made to the Far East (Hong Kong, Taiwan and Mainland China). My wife, Ina, and I met during this period, and the collection of Chinese Glass continued to expand despite a relocation to Kansas City in the early 1980's.

During the initial 15 years I was collecting Chinese glass, very little current published material on the subject was available to provide a framework for making intelligent and well informed collecting decisions. However three excellent, comprehensive exhibition featuring Qing period Chinese glass have been held during the last ten years, each of which has resulted in an outstanding catalogue being published. All three catalogues (the two earliest ones unfortunately out of print) not only describe the collections exhibited but, also, present excellent articles by scholars in the field examining the history, chronology and technology of Chinese glass making. Most illustrations were rendered in color, and between all three groupings, over 250 individual pieces of Chinese glass were published, thus providing an excellent reference framework from which collectors can evaluate similar pieces. Acquiring and studying these catalogues is virtually a "must" if someone is seriously interested in learning more about the subject.

Claudia Brown, Curator of Asian Art at the Phoenix Art Museum in Arizona, and her late husband, *Donald Rabiner*, a former professor at Arizona State University, cooperated in doing the remarkable research and writing that produced most of the written materials published in all three exhibit catalogues. I would like to take this opportunity, on behalf of myself and all collectors of Chinese glass, to thank Claudia for these three outstanding works and to commend her for increasing the field of knowledge and focusing public interest on this exciting subject, Qing period Chinese glass.

Fortunately, frequent nationwide travel (and some overseas travel as well) necessitated by my executive search business allowed Chinese Glass acquisitions to be made ranging from Seattle to Miami, Boston to San Diego, and London to Hong Kong. Today the entire collection exceeds 200 pieces , although not all would necessarily be of the high quality of those being exhibited.

Almost all of the Chinese Glass in the collection was acquired from Oriental Antiques dealers (at their shops), Auction houses, Antiques shows (particularly those where Oriental Antiques dealers participated), and, occasionally, at an Antiques mall. Many of the choicest pieces were purchased as gifts from the two most important women in my life: my wife, Ina, and my mother, Elizabeth, both of whom much admire Chinese Glass. Their thoughtfulness and their generosity over the years have been appreciated very much,

About one-half the pieces in this exhibition were previously displayed at the Lentz Center for Asian Culture, University of Nebraska Museum, Lincoln, from October 21, 1994 through January 14, 1995. That exhibit was entitled "Chinese Glass:

Bounties of the Qing: The Hilmes-Gadient Collection of Chinese Glass." *Philip and Margaret Hilmes* were also serious collectors of Chinese Glass, and became close friends while sharing their extensive knowledge on the subject with me. I am especially grateful for their assistance and friendship over many years. This relationship has fueled both of our interest in adding to our respective collections.

Questions frequently asked are: "How do you know that a particular piece of glass is Chinese?" and "What determines the quality of any individual specimen?" Nine characteristics are typically examined during the acquisition process: shape (form) of the piece (does it look Chinese?); texture of the glass (older Chinese glass frequently has a "greasy" feel and often contains impurities); color of the glass itself (is it a typical Chinese color?); weight of the glass (older Chinese glass is frequently very heavy – not unlike leaded crystal); foot-rim (base) design and finish (must be consistent with Chinese methods); top-rim design and finish, including the hollowing and finish of the opening; if carved, subject-matter of design (is it typically Chinese); and carving quality (is it consistent with methods used during time period of production?). If these eight characteristics pass muster, then the reign mark (seal) – if it is a marked piece – is closely examined to determine if it seems appropriate to the period designated, both in style of the inscribed Chinese characters and workmanship. Since many skilled glass artisans rotated between the Imperial Glass Workshop, on the Palace grounds, and their own glass works, it is possible to find almost identical pieces with one bearing a reign mark while the other is unmarked. This alone should in no way detract from the quality of the unsigned piece,

This exhibit and catalog have been accomplished primarily through the efforts of *Susie and François Lorin*, owners of Asiantiques in Winter Park, Florida. Little did I realize some ten years ago, when I purchased an Imperial Yellow Chinese Glass vase from them at a New Orleans Antiques Show, what good friends and supporters they would become over future years. The Lorin's integrity and professionalism in Asian Antiquities is well respected throughout the Nation, and I would like to thank them personally for their support and encouragement that have caused this exhibition to reach fruition.

Many well known collectors of Oriental Antiques who have amassed famous collections (and who were undoubtedly both wiser and wealthier than I am) utilize Consultants, Advisers, and even Museum Curators to assist them in making group decisions to acquire the objects comprising their notable collections. In my case, I have personally selected each piece in this exhibit, and I have relied upon no one else to collaborate with in making the buying decisions. Thus, I want to assume full responsibility for any shortcoming in the individual pieces exhibited.

Having enjoyed collecting glass over the past 25 years, and being 61 years of age, it is my hope and expectation (with the Good Lord's help) to continue collecting it for another 25 years.

Sincerely,

Sandford Gadient
Boca Raton, Florida

Acknowledgments

This catalogue has been prepared for an exhibition of selected Chinese glass pieces from the collection of Ina and Sandford Gadient. The exhibition encompasses but a fraction from the collection and the examples shown were chosen at random to represent a significant sample of the entire collection. It was, therefore, interesting to find out that more than half of the items selected date to the 18th century or earlier in the Qing dynasty and that twelve of them bear a mark attributable with certainty to the Yongzheng or the Qianlong period.

First and foremost we want to thank *Ina* and *Sandford Gadient* for their patient quest that has lead to the formation of such a varied and remarkable collection. We also want to thank them for their confidence in our ability to present their objects as our premier exhibit and catalogue in our new Winter Park Gallery. Ina and Sandford did not hesitate to accept when we offered them to set up the exhibit at the occasion of the Imperial Tombs of China exhibition coming to the Orlando Museum of Art during the summer 1997.

Chinese glass is an interesting subject. Except for three major exhibitions held in the United States during the last eight years, limited amounts of comprehensive studies have been written about it. And, to this point, the wealth of knowledge to be drawn from the study of Chinese glass snuff bottles has, for most part, been overlooked.

At the same time there is a strong interest in every form of art glass in our community of Winter Park, Florida – immediately adjacent to Orlando – where the Morse Museum of American Art hosts one of the largest collection of Tiffany glass in the nation less than two blocks from our gallery. It is at the occasion of a lecture on Chinese glass that we were invited to give there last January that the idea of this exhibition came about as our way to salute the wonderful introduction to Chinese art that the Orlando Museum of Art is bringing to Central Florida with its summer presentation.

Many have contributed to this exhibition and to its catalogue. It is our pleasure to thank them here.

Thank you to *Clarence Shangraw* for enthusiastically agreeing to write the introduction to the catalogue and for doing it so precisely. His understanding of the subject and review of the collection are much appreciated. Further, we thank *Clarence Shangraw* for being so gracious and understanding regarding our strict publication deadlines.

Thank you to *Jana Volf* for undertaking the difficult task of writing the entries in the catalogue, scrutinizing each piece to find its least apparent qualities (and sometimes its flaws!), patiently tracking every comparable pieces and describing each vessel (vase, bowl, censer,...) in detail and with accuracy. Being a scholar in the field of Chinese snuff bottles, Jana has acquired a considerable familiarity with Chinese glass and provides here a somewhat different perspective on the subject than previous writers. We know how much she wished to have more time to research more comparable items, enrich her comments with more insights on more pieces and we know how right she was to want to do so. In spite of our time constraints she is offering a meaningful contribution to the knowledge of Chinese glass and we are proud of the end result of her considerable efforts and expertise.

Thank you to *Raymond Martinot* for the quality of his photographs and his patience in accepting to shoot the objects. He has worked for many prestigious institutions in the past – including the *Louvres Museum* – and we feel honored to have him as our friend and our photographer.

Thank you to our friend and partner, *Paul Markunas,* for materially setting up the exhibition, designing its cases, choosing its lighting and coordinating its advertising and communication. Through the years we have always had the greatest confidence in Paul's abilities as an outstanding designer and communicator. As usual, he has outdone himself.

Thank you to *Philippe Lorin* for devoting his efforts to the production of the catalogue, a very small project for his company, *Lec. communication, in Paris.* The talented professionals who work so closely with him, particularly *Anne Chaponnay* in Paris for the design, have made our dream come true in spite of all the difficulties generated by the distances and the tight time frame. They deserve to be particularly thanked for it. *Philippe* has kept us all on track and has accepted to do the impossible for the catalogue to be published for the opening of the exhibition. Thank you again: it is a grand job!

And thank you to *Jeffrey Moy* and *Art Media Resources in Chicago* for guiding us through the "formalities" of publishing and for committing to distribute this catalogue throughout the art publications community.

Susie and **François Lorin**
Asiantiques, Inc.

Introduction

Chinese Monochrome Glass of the Qing Dynasty (1644-1912)

Clarence F. Shangraw
Chief Curator Emeritus, Asian Art Museum of San Francisco.
Director Emeritus, Tsui Museum of Art, Hong Kong.

By the 2nd century BC. several small regional centers of glass production were widely distributed throughout north and south China. Some endured, some did not, as over the centuries the demands of the patron changed and evolved, with foreign glasses, particularly those of Central Asian and Southwest Asian origins, impacting on the Chinese glass industry. Thus, Chinese glass making never did thrive at a production level with, nor with the status of, wares of the ceramics and porcelain industry. Nevertheless it did, although without continuous evolution, sporadically pulse in development, the glass makers of the north preferring to make opaque and translucent wares, those of the south transparent and semi-transparent or translucent items. That pattern persists until the 14th century when two formerly regional centers take dominance in glassmaking, establishing themselves as concentrated hubs that can now be evaluated on evidence from present-day archeological retrieval and an examination of then-contemporary historical texts.

Canton (now Guangzhou in Guandong province) developed into the southern center, while in the north it was the legendary home of Chinese glassmaking, Boshan in Shandong province. The so-called Peking glass, a misnomer of sorts as glass was not extensively worked there (except in the 18th and 19th century imperial glasshouse) but in the Boshan area. Glass rods from Boshan could be transported to any regional glass-finishing studio, which did occur, thus it is more accurate to avoid the term Peking glass, except in specific reference to Qing imperial glass.

The early development of glass coincides with contemporaneous Daoist practices with alchemy, primarily by choosing inorganic materials found in Nature that are then combined and altered by heat and fire to create a man-made, synthetic material. At the time, it was thought that the newly created substance was imbued with pseudo-scientific significance symbolically capable of averting evil or even guaranteeing immortality. This associationship between glass and its derivatives inspirations from Nature, emphatically gemstones, minerals, and crystals weave a constant, close-knit union that persists throughout glass history in China. The earliest mention of this interaction occurs in the official history of the Han dynasty (*2nd century BC. - 2nd century AD.*), noting that glass had become used as a faux gem. Also, in Tang times (*618-906 AD.*) texts mention a transparent, clear glass that is likened to rock crystal. The latter is known as the "water-gem" and believed to be petrified ice because of its tenacious longevity from any altered state and thus the material must have extensive magical and healing powers. By Song times (*960-1279 AD.*), the inspiration from Nature expands beyond the petrologic world to find descriptive, lyrical color terms, especially selected hues like "duck's egg green" and "gosling yellow." In the Chinese world, their sense of color is derived from Nature, and not from the scientific spectrum as done in the Western world. It is thus a more intuitive, empirical approach to qualifying colors, hues, tinges and tints. Even as early as the 2nd century B. C. in China's first dictionary, Lhe Shuo-wen, the color-term qing is defined as "the color of Nature in distance," thus embracing a broad tonality range of greens, blues, q and tans. The word for blue-and-white porcelain, (qinghua) literally meaning "blue flowers," embraces this color term. It thus becomes distinctly clear that Chinese glass and the broad extent of Nature, and everything that world can provide as creative inspiration for the glass-maker, are very much intertwined and united.

During the Qing dynasty glassmaking comes under Imperial patronage for the first and only time in China's history. A most visionary ruler, the Kangxi Emperor (*r. 1662-1722*) established by edict an Imperial Glasshouse in 1696 within the precincts of the Forbidden City as part of his extensive Department of Imperial Artwork Studios. These studios supplied the Palace with its needs and furnishings, provided highest quality objects for the imperial families, and met the throne's request for court paraphernalia, diplomatic gifts and tribute wares. Initially imperial glass was heavily imbued with westernizations, primarily technical construction and working methods, due to the presence of European missionaries at court; but after two decades of such experimentation and wonderment it became short-lived without any lasting influence on the glass made during the remainder of the 18th century. The glass makers reverted to more familiar, more native traditions, and when they did they launched, through their initiative and creative genius, the Golden Age of Glassmaking in China that persisted to the end of that century. This occurred during the reign of Kangxi's son Yongzheng (*r. 1723-35*) and grandson Qianlong (*r. 1736-96*).

Qing glass was worked with many different techniques and with extensive experimentation with color and combination of colors, however the monochrome tradition did dominate. An object could be blown, molded, or carved from a block with the same working approach as the jade lapidary. Once shaped it could be reheated and mavered (rolled in a semi-molten state) on a flat surface to perfect the form or to add by mavering powdered, or minutely pulverized surface particles of a contrasting or a complementary shade that makes the applied layer appear as a mere gossamer film. With the latter approach a favorite of the glassmakers was an emulation of the contemporary, imperial peachbloom glaze on porcelains, an example of which appears in this exhibition.

Chinese glass monochromes come in a broad array of colors, over thirty having been registered in the Palace records. Included are opaque white, seashell white, yolk yellow, pale yellow, realgar orange, coral, transparent tea-green, transparent tea-yellow likened to eel's belly yellow, moonglow white, cobalt blue, light sky-blue, dark ruby-red, mallow-rose pink, peachbloom red, pea green, light green, kidney bean reddish purple, amethyst purple, jasperish brownish red, smoky quartz crystal and kingfisher feather blue. Yellow was the Qing imperial color and thus the most popular of the monochromes. Its range of intensity extends from a pale, frothy and light shade to more imbued, sombre and rich variations resembling yolk. Other favorites were a deep and rich cobalt blue most often with a shimmering violet tinge, a deep and luscious red as rich as the copper red glazes on contemporary porcelains, and the variety of whites. The latter were never starkly white as white as a color is associated with death (the hueless state of being) and therefore the Chinese preference for whites with softly tinted tones, particularly a softly warm opalescent tinge, probably inspired by the purity and color of nephrite jades. As they had through their history, Qing glassmakers continued to emulate the colors and textures of natural materials, such as minerals, thereby creating colorful works. These were created out of playfulness and with humor and were simple exercises to boast of one's mastery of mineralogical colors. They were merely created within the realm of artistic conceit rather than any deceit.

The monochrome glass colors of that Golden Age had never been in their artistic repertory prior to that time, and once the age starts declining in the early 19th century this colorful chorus line of visual enjoyment passes into oblivion. Nevertheless, some of the objects do survive reminding posterity of that glorious time in the history of Chinese glass.

Catalogue

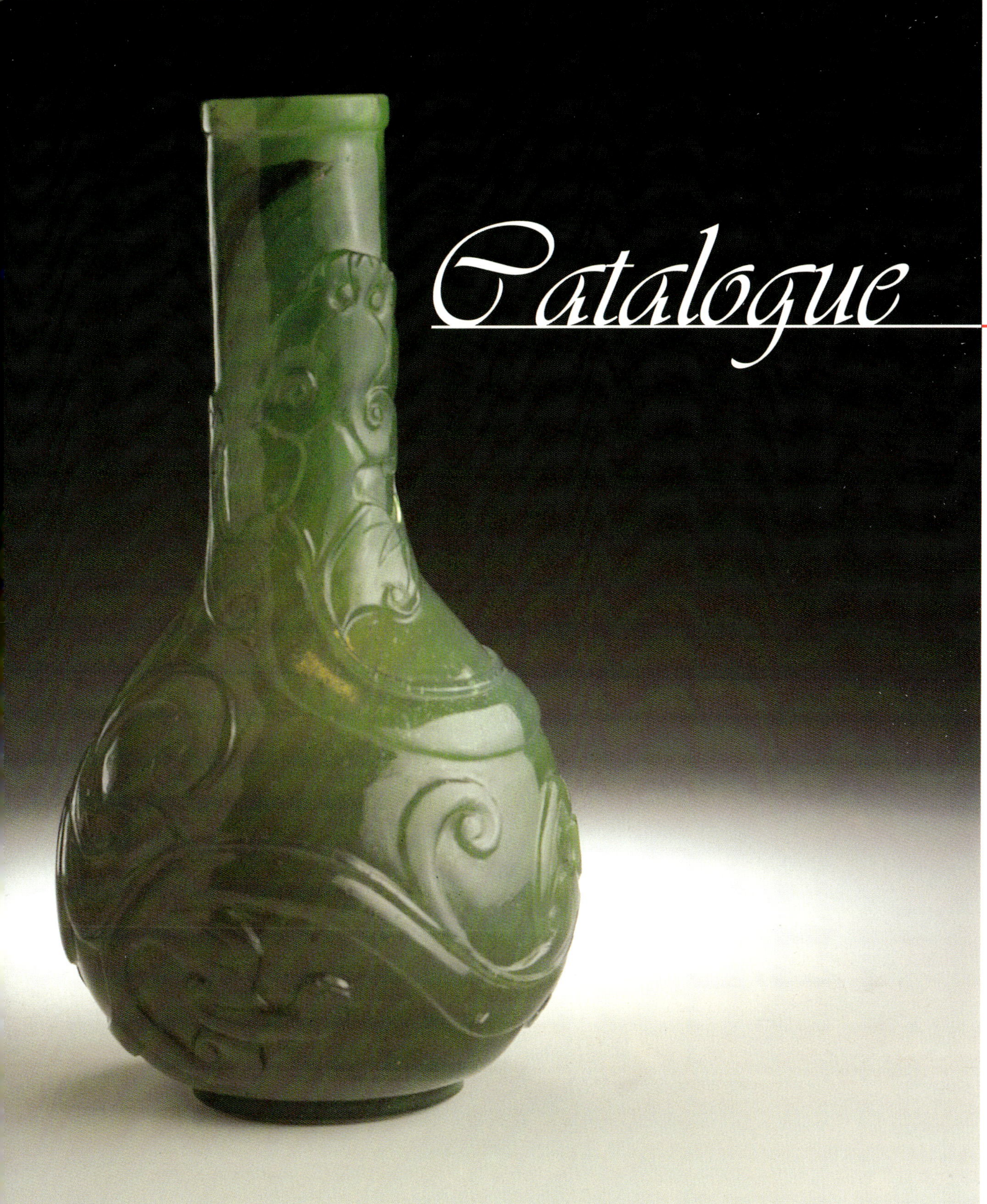

I

Small vase

Colorless glass imitating rock crystal
Qing dynasty, 18 th century
H: 11,9 cm

The ovoid body of this small vase is carved in high relief with a continuous design of flowers and rock work. Both the narrow edges are distinguished by a single, fantastic rock. The body is supported on a high foot ring that surrounds a deeply recessed base. The neck is gently flared and has a wide rim. The thick and heavy colorless glass has only a few tiny bubbles. The appearance and weight of the glass closely resemble rock crystal.

Colorless glass made as an intentional imitation of rock crystal appears to be one of the early types of glass produced in the Qing period. Palace records document that by the Yongzheng period glass was used in place of gems for official insignia and that a fifth-class officer would use clear glass in place of rock crystal in the top-knot of his hat (see *Yang Boda*, ***"A Brief Account of Qing Dynasty Glass"*** *in Claudia Brown and Donald Rabiner*, ***Chinese Glass of the Qing Dynasty, 1644-1911: The Robert H. Clague Collection***, *exhibition catalogue, Phoenix Art museum, 1987, page 72).*

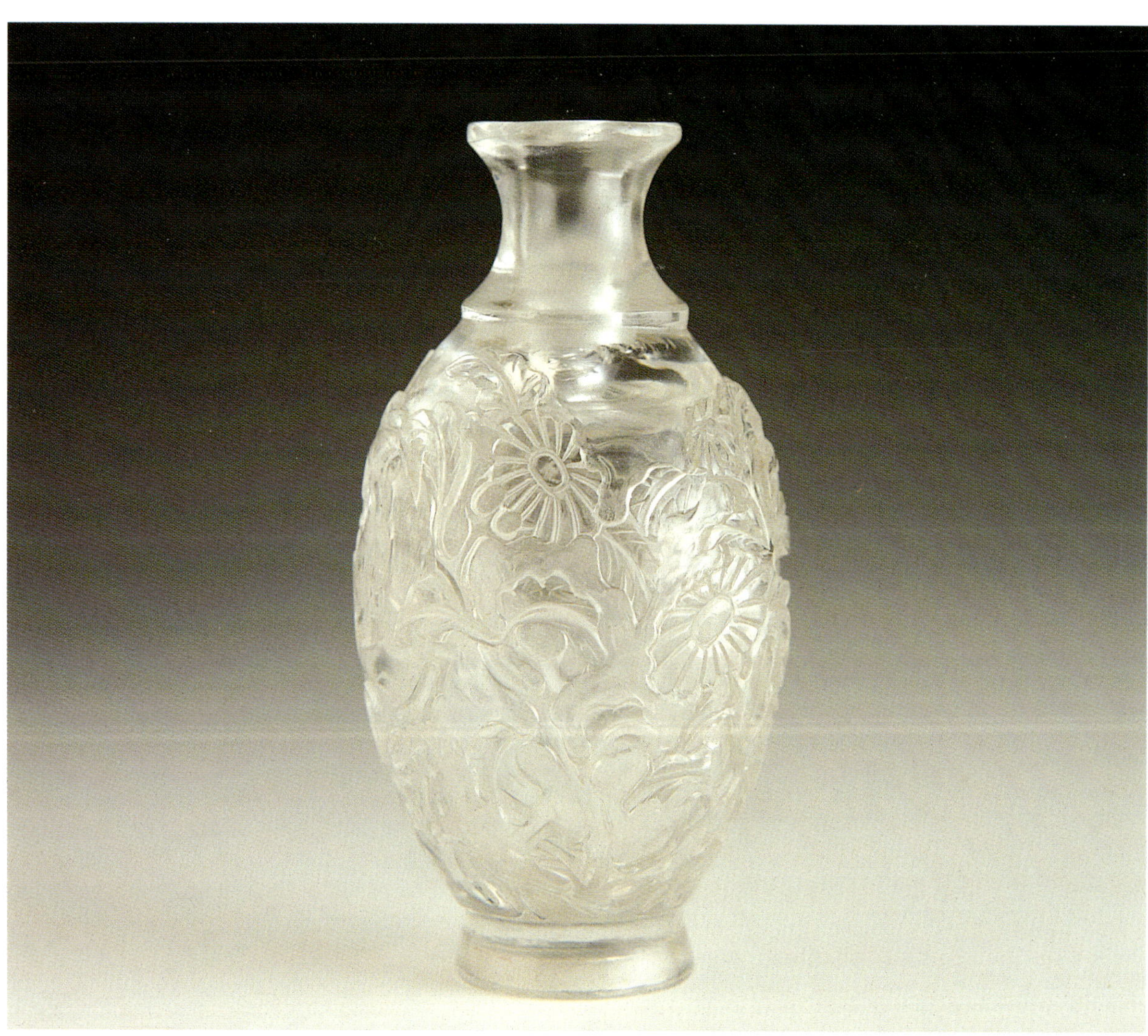

2

Bottle

Opaque white glass
Qing dynasty, Qianlong mark and period, 1736-95
H: 12,3 cm

This **bottle** is formed from two separate layers of glass, a pale green-white color entirely covering a more opaque white ground. The full, ovoid body has large bulging shoulders that ascend to a short, cylindrical neck. The body is supported on an extremely short foot ring. The mark **Qianlong nian zhi** is carved in shallow relief in seal script on the flat base. There is some minor pitting to the exterior surface as well as a fairly large black inclusion on the base.

Cased or overlay glass (glass in which one color has been fused to the surface of another) is most often associated with the carved cameo style examples, especially those with a white or colorless ground covered by a single transparent red or blue glass (such as n° 34 in the collection). The present jar, however, is also an example of cased glass as the lip clearly indicates that the vessel is formed from two separate layers of glass even though the bottom layer is not visible on the exterior. This type of cased glass is called **su tao** (plain overlay) in Chinese (see *Yang Boda*, ***"A Brief Account of Qing Dynasty Glass"*** in *Claudia Brown and Donald Rabiner*, ***Chinese Glass of the Qing Dynasty, 1644-1911: The Robert H. Clague Collection***, *exhibition catalogue, Phoenix Art Museum, 1987, page 77)*.

A jar of closely related shape, but carved with a lotus leaf and petal design is in the collection of Mrs. Barney Dagen (see *Clarence Shangraw and Claudia Brown*, ***A Chorus of Colors: Chinese Glass from Three American Collections***, *exhibition catalogue, Asian Art Museum of San Francisco, 1995, page 58, cat. n° 30)*.

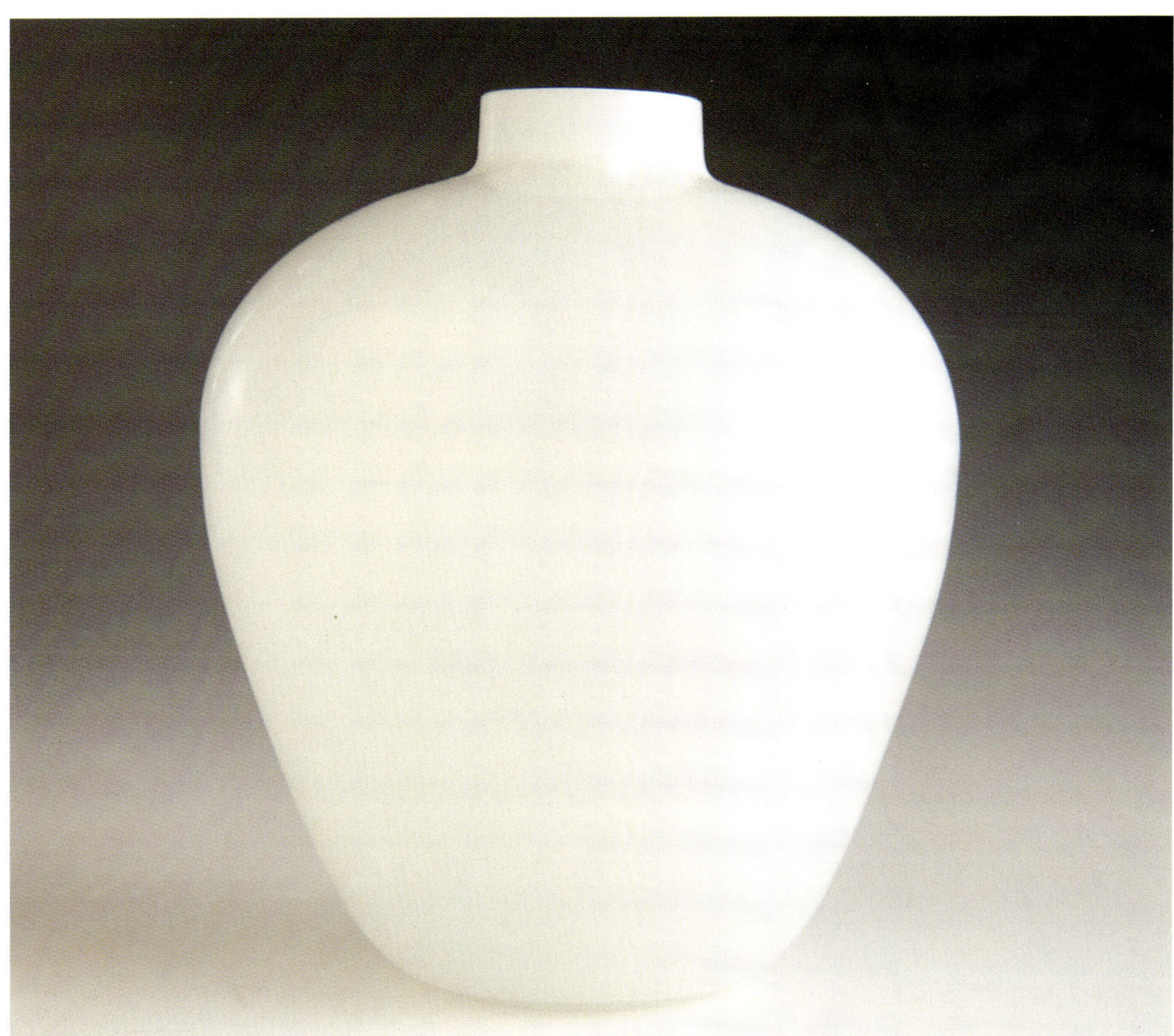

3

Vase

Opaque yellow-white glass
Qing dynasty, 18 th century
H: 23,1 cm

Formed of thick glass this tall, slender vase has a lightly swollen body from which rises the long, nearly cylindrical neck. The high foot ring is formed from a thick coil of glass and is applied to the body. The glass is of warm, yellow-white color with some thin striations of lighter tone as well as numerous bubbles and small inclusions throughout.

A vase also formed from unusually thick glass and of related shape, but lacking a foot ring and of opaque blue-green color is in the collection of Alan E. Feen (see *Clarence Shangraw and Claudia Brown, **A Chorus of Colors: Chinese Glass from Three American Collections**, exhibition catalogue, Asian Art Museum of San Francisco, 1995, page 81, cat. n° 50)*. The example in the Feen Collection includes the wheel engraved mark **Qianlong nian zhi** on the base.

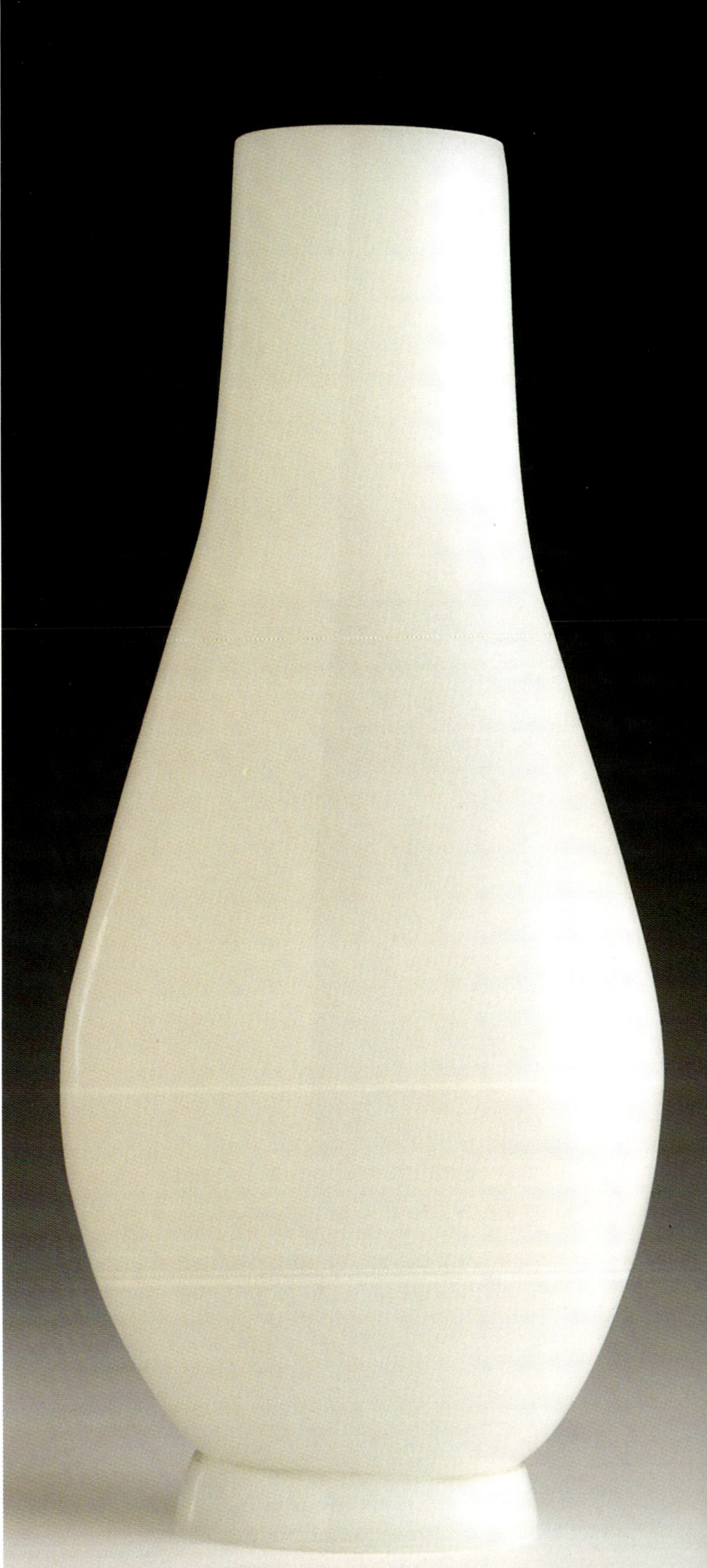

4

Bowl

Opaque white glass imitating
blanc de Chine *porcelain*
Qing dynasty, 18 th century
H: 18,3 cm

This beautifully formed bowl has rounded, gently flared walls that ascend to an everted rim. The body is formed from a fairly thick, opaque white glass that is smooth as well as highly lustrous and remarkably similar in appearance to blanc de Chine porcelain. The bowl is supported on a relatively high foot ring. The underside of the foot ring is mat and has a slightly rough texture so as to imitate the surface of an unglazed foot on a porcelain example. The base is deeply recessed.

Glass imitations of porcelain shapes and/or glazes are fairly common in Qing dynasty glass. It is, however, fairly unusual to find such a carefully copied and meticulously finished example as the present bowl. The remarkable accuracy in which this bowl is rendered is perhaps more pronounced if one compares it, even through photographs, to a blanc de Chine porcelain example (*see P. J. Donnelly*, ***Blanc de Chine***, *London, 1969, plate 3a*).

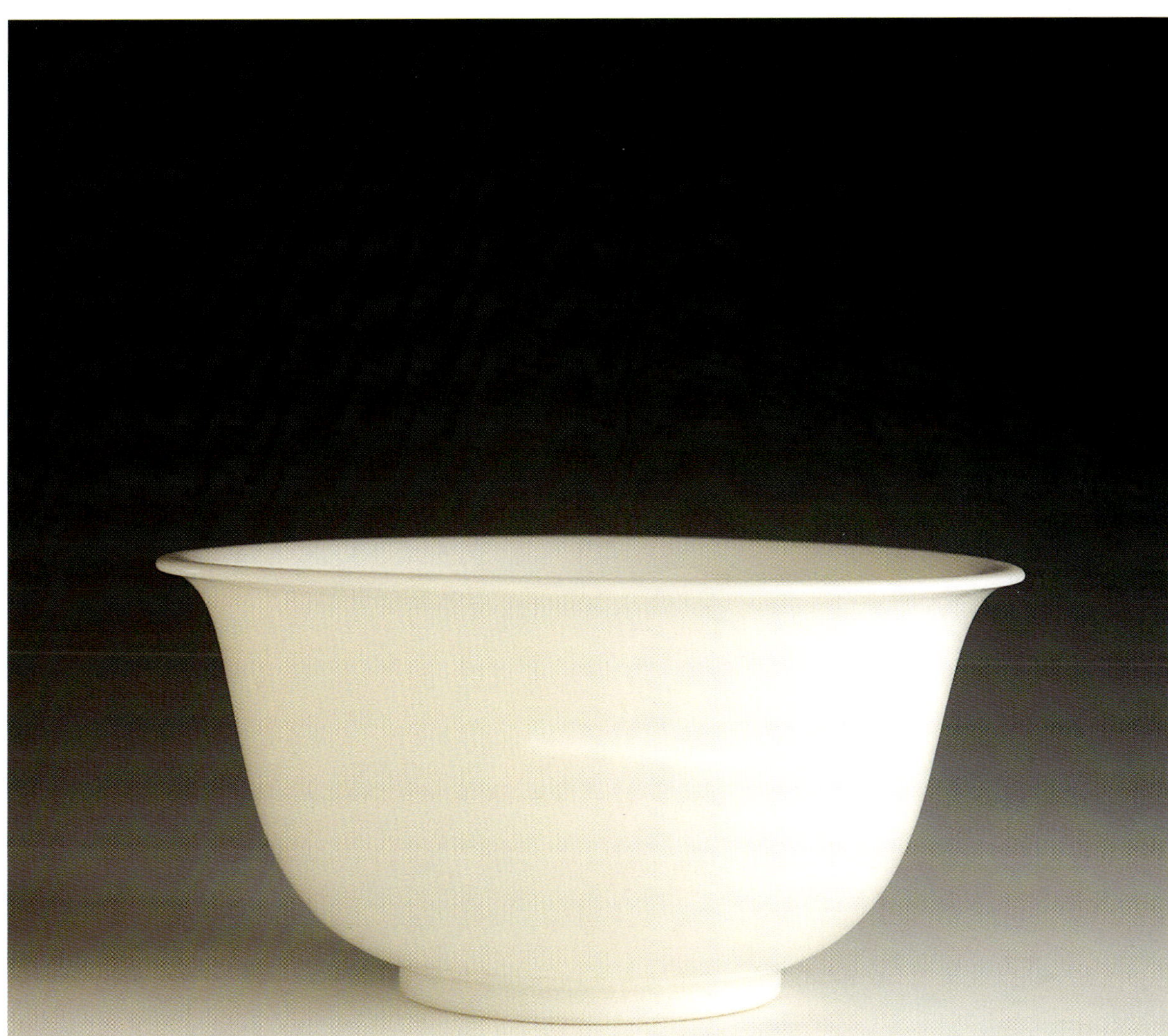

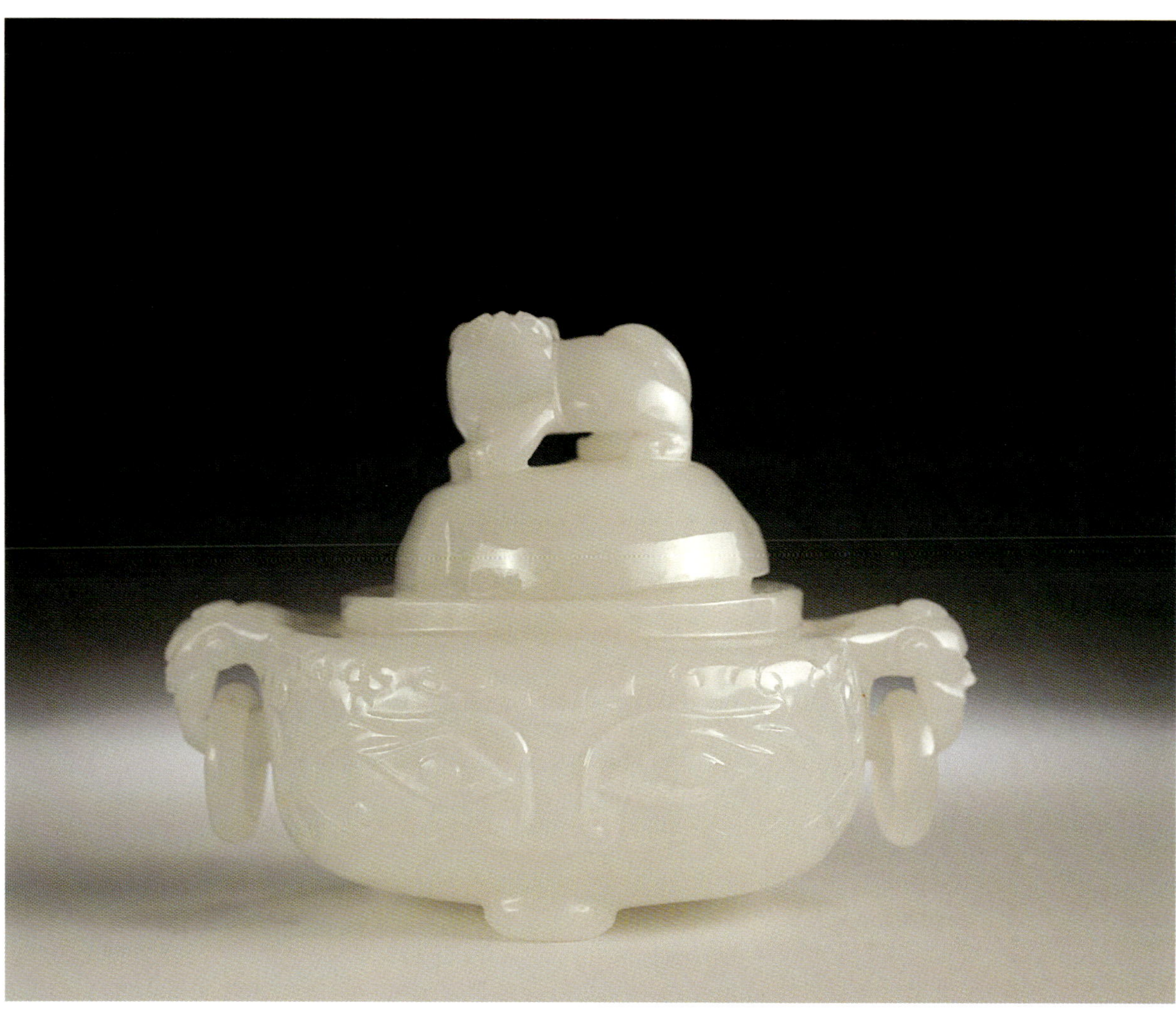

5

Covered censer

Opaque white glass imitating nephrite
Qing dynasty, 19 th century
H: 7,8 cm

This **tripod incense burner** is formed from a fairly thick, opaque glass that is of consistent white tone. The exterior surface of the jade-like glass is boldly carved in low relief with two **taotie** masks below a wide rim. The loop handles are carved as animal heads of ferocious appearance. From each handle is suspended a loose ring carved from the same glass. The dome shape cover is surmounted by a small Buddhist lion which forms the knob.

The **taotie** mask motif and the animal head form handles represented on the present example are adopted from those on ancient bronze vessels. The **taotie** mask was an especially favorite motif in the decorative arts of the Qing period. It was commonly used on glass as well as porcelain and jade. For example a closely related **taotie** mask can be found on a Kangxi porcelain square shape censer that also includes a Buddhist lion form knob in the Collection of the Palace Museum, Beijing (*see*, ***Kangxi, Yongzheng and Qianlong Qing Porcelain from the Palace Museum Collection***, *Beijing, Forbidden City Publishing House, The Woods Publishing Co., 1989, n° 65*).

For a covered censer carved with **taotie** mask motifs as well as loop handles but of opaque pink glass imitating coral see Claudia Brown and Donald Rabiner, ***Chinese Glass of the Qing Dynasty, 1644-1911: The Robert H. Clague Collection***, *exhibition catalogue, Phoenix Art Museum, 1987, page 41, n° 41.*

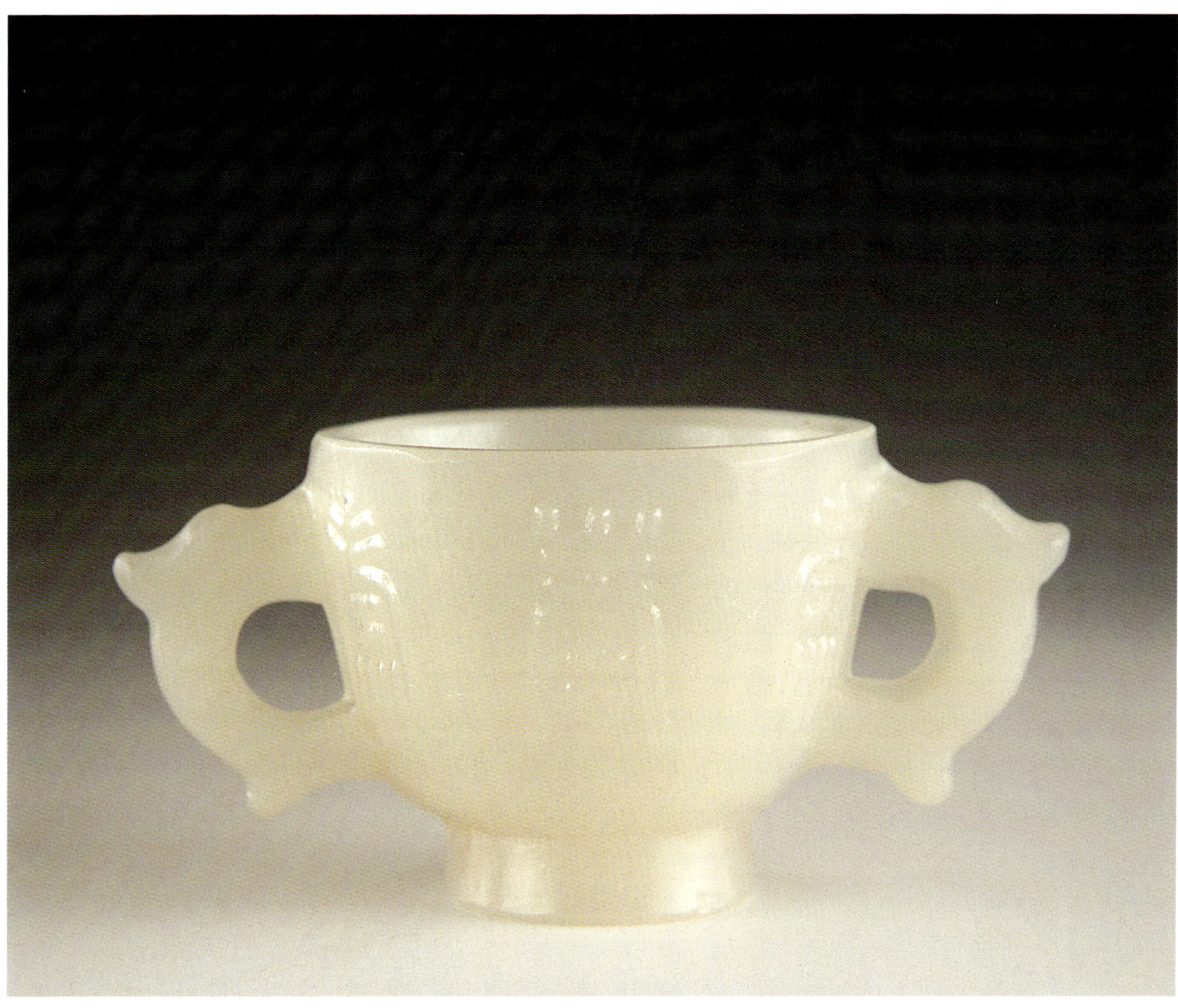

6

Two-handled cup with *shou* (long life) characters

Opaque green-white glass imitating nephrite
Ming to early Qing dynasty, 17 th century
H: 5,5 cm

T**his hexagonal cup** was fashioned by molding rather than by carving. Traces of the mold are still evident in the form of a thin seam on both the narrow sides as well as on the interior edge of the loop handles. Each of the six panels has the character **shou** (long life) molded in relief. The handles are formed as abstract animal heads and no interior details, such as the eyes, are rendered. The cup is supported on a high foot ring. The fairly thick glass is of green-white color and resembles jade in its appearance as well as in its weight.

Cups closely related in shape, decoration and material appear in several collections; see Clarence Shangraw and Claudia Brown, ***A Chorus of Colors: Chinese Glass from Three American Collections***, *exhibition catalogue, Asian Art Museum of San Francisco, 1995, page 42, cat. n° 16* from the collection of Walter and Phyllis Shorenstein *and also page 43, cat. n° 17* from the collection of Alan E. Feen. For a related example, but of square shape, see Claudia Brown and Donald Rabiner, ***Chinese Glass of the Qing Dynasty, 1644-1911: The Robert H. Clague Collection***, *exhibition catalogue, Phoenix Art Museum, 1987, page 62, cat. n° 74.*

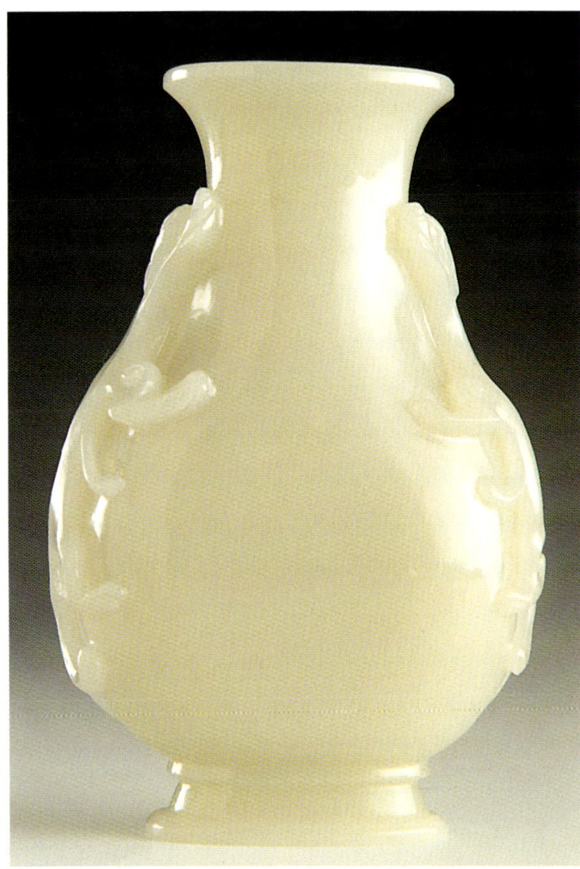

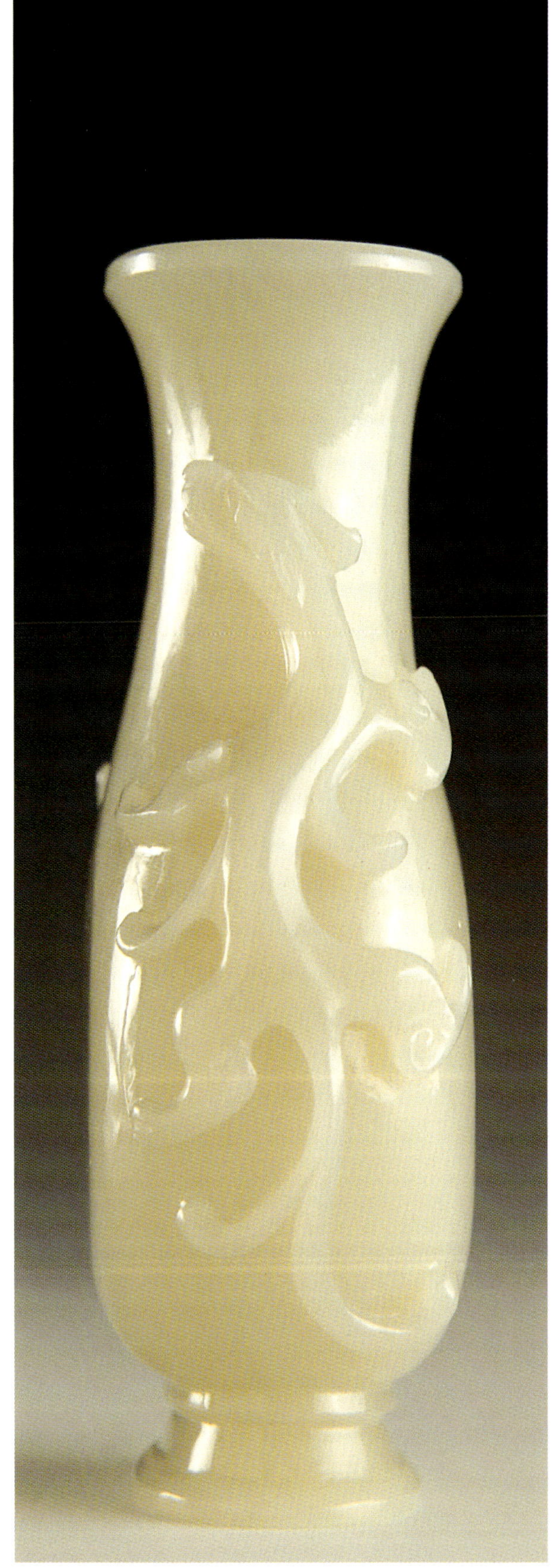

7

Vase of *hu* shape

Opaque yellow-white glass imitating nephrite
Qing dynasty, 18 th century
H: 11,7 cm

This elegant *hu*-shape vase is formed from a thick, opaque yellow-white glass that closely resembles jade in appearance and in weight. The surface of the glass is smooth and lustrous. The neck is gracefully flared and has a deeply concave lip with a relatively small, circular mouth. Each narrow side is exquisitely carved in high relief with a **zhilong** that appears to climb up the edge of the vase. Both **zhilong** have their head turned toward the same main side. The body is supported on a high foot of oval shape with a fairly thick rounded lower edge. The underside of the foot is finely crafted with a fairly wide outer foot ring as well as a second one, thinner, which is slightly recessed. The base itself is deeply recessed.

The design and workmanship of this ***hu***-shape vase share much in common with jade carving of the eighteenth century. It is, in fact, very likely that this glass vase was not only modeled after an actual nephrite example, but also that it was carved by jade workers. The high quality of the carving, the precision with which the carving as well as the form imitate a jade piece and the vase's overall elegant appearance suggest that it is a product of the palace workshop.

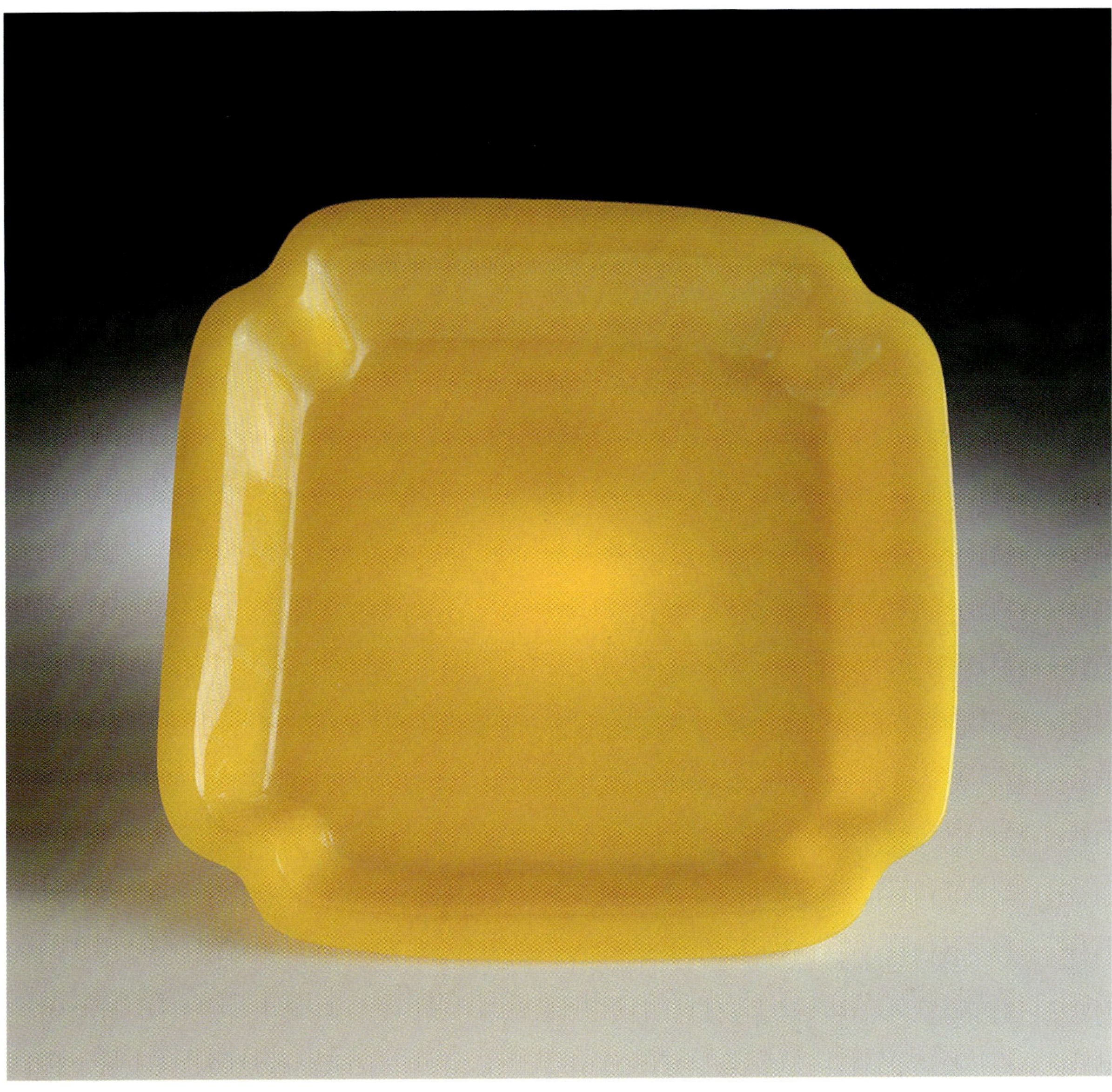

8

Square tray with chamfered corners

Crizzled opaque yellow glass
Qing dynasty, 18 th century
H: 17,3 cm

Vessels carved with **zhilong** clinging to their sides are relatively common in jade: see *James C. Y. Watt, **Chinese Jades from Han to Ch'ing**, exhibition catalogue, The Asia Society, New York, 1980, page 134, n° 111*. **Zhilong** are also a common subject on glass wares, but it is quite rare to find the primary subject on larger glass pieces represented only on the narrow sides of the vessel. There is, however, a rather small group of glass snuff bottles, mostly made in imitation of various semi-precious stones such as emerald and aquamarine, which are carved with **zhilong** on the narrow sides: see ***Zhongguo biyanhu zhenshang***, edited by *Geng Baochang and Zhao Binghua, Hong Kong, Joint Publishing and Taikong Culture Enterprise, 1992, page 67, n° 48.*

T**his relatively deep tray** has fairly thick walls that are slightly flared and ascend to a wide, everted rim. The four gently rounded corners are indented and their shape dictates the outward bulge on the corners in the interior of the tray. The square base is flat. The glass is of opaque deep yellow color. The color is consistent throughout the piece, however, there is extensive crizzling on the interior surface which gives the yellow color an uneven appearance.

9

Vase of hexagonal section

Opaque yellow glass
Qing dynasty, 18 th century
H: 9,8 cm

This elegant vase has a body that gently tapers toward the base and is divided into six panels. The panels are clearly defined by sharp, vertical ridges on the long sides and by a rounded upper edge, so that each resembles a flower petal. The shoulders are of small, well rounded form and gracefully rise to a short, flared neck. The body is supported on an extremely short foot of hexagonal shape. The size and shape of the foot give the vase an appearance of almost floating above the surface on which it stands. The glass is of opaque deep yellow color and has a heavily pitted surface as well as numerous bubbles and inclusions throughout.

Yellow glass is mentioned in court records as early as 1705 (see *Yang Boda, "A Brief Account of Qing Dynasty Glass", in Claudia Brown and Donald Rabiner,* ***Chinese Glass of the Qing Dynasty, 1644-1911: The Robert H. Clague Collection****, exhibition catalogue, Phoenix Art Museum, 1987, page 77*). The Palace Museum in Beijing has only twelve Yongzheng mark and period glass pieces in its collection and of these four are of yellow color. What is especially interesting and quite remarkable about these four Yongzheng glass pieces is that each is described as a different yellow: light yellow, yellow, deep yellow and translucent yellow (see *Yang Boda, as cited above, page 78*). This suggests that already by the Yongzheng period a varied and sophisticated range of yellow tones had been developed. The fascination with and development of yellow color glass was an important aspect of eighteenth century Chinese glass production and one that is distinctly Chinese in character as one does not find a parallel interest or development in the European glass making tradition for it.

The heavily pitted surface and the numerous small black inclusions throughout the glass of this small vase are characteristic of early Qing glass and suggest a Yongzheng or early Qianlong date for this piece. The extremely elegant shape of the vase and its slightly delicate appearance are also consistent with an early eighteenth century date.

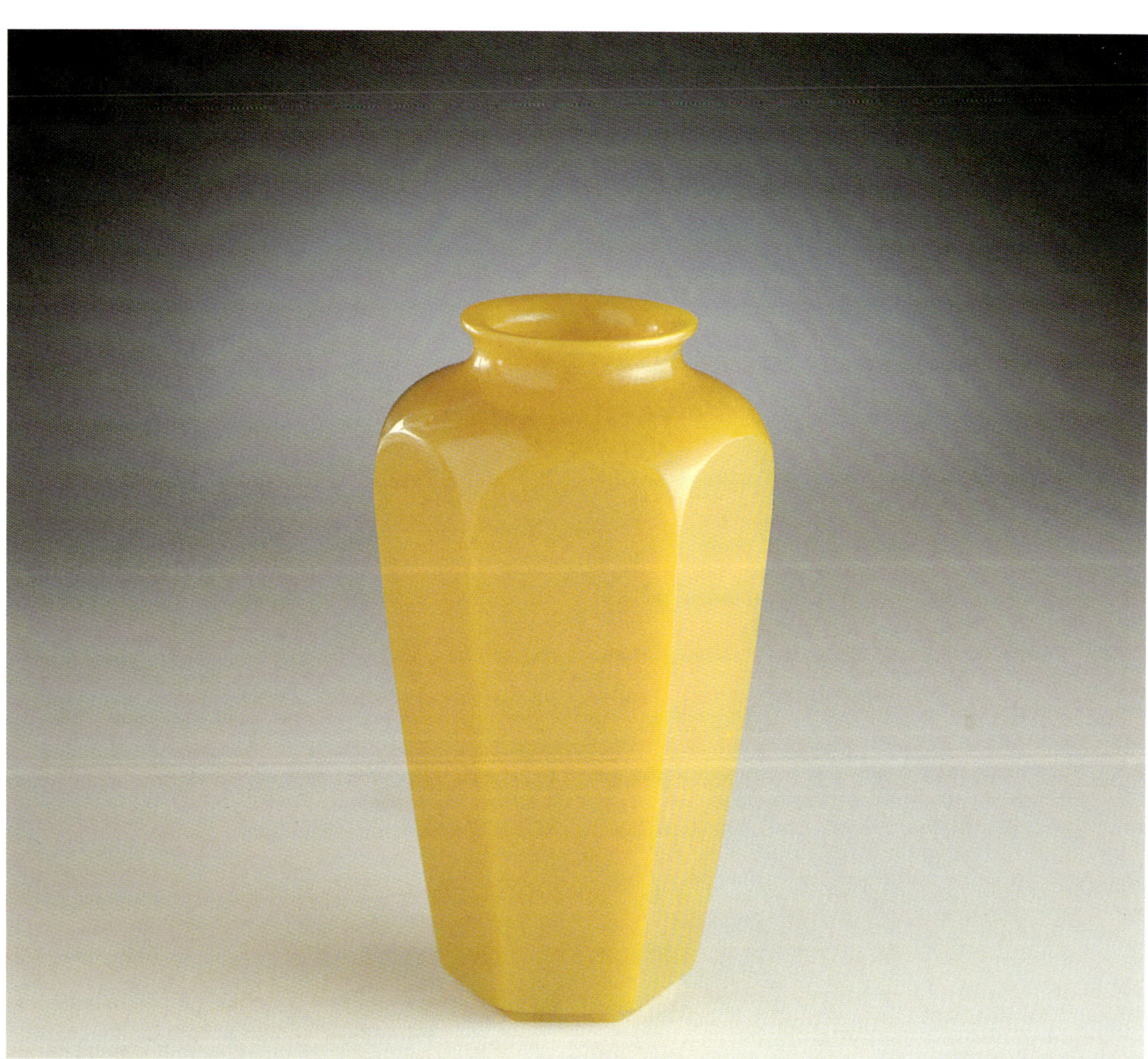

10

Gourd-shaped water dropper

Opaque yellow glass
Qing dynasty, 18 th century
H: 12,1 cm

The **well formed body** of this water dropper is carved as a double-gourd, with a compressed lower bulb and a more elongated, slightly ovoid shape upper bulb. The long, thin neck is of nearly cylindrical shape except for the upper portion of one side which is very subtly curved inward. The mouth is of oval shape with its smallest point corresponding to the curved side of the neck. The circular base is flat. The fairly thick glass is of opaque deep yellow color and has a slightly waxy surface. This vessel is surprisingly heavy for its size.

In shape and material this piece is closely related to a vessel in the collection of Walter and Phyllis Shorenstein (see, *Clarence Shangraw and Claudia Brown, **A Chorus of Colors: Chinese Glass from Three American Collections**, exhibition catalogue, Asian Art Museum of San Francisco, 1995, page 92, cat. n° 64*). The Shorenstein example, however, has a shorter and thinner neck that gracefully bends toward one side.

Claudia Brown in her commentary on the Shorenstein piece suggests that it may have been intended to be used as a water dropper. The present example's oval shape lip with its spout-like tip as well as the very subtle inward curve on one side of the neck to accommodate the thumb when pouring confirm the identification of both vessels function as a water dropper.

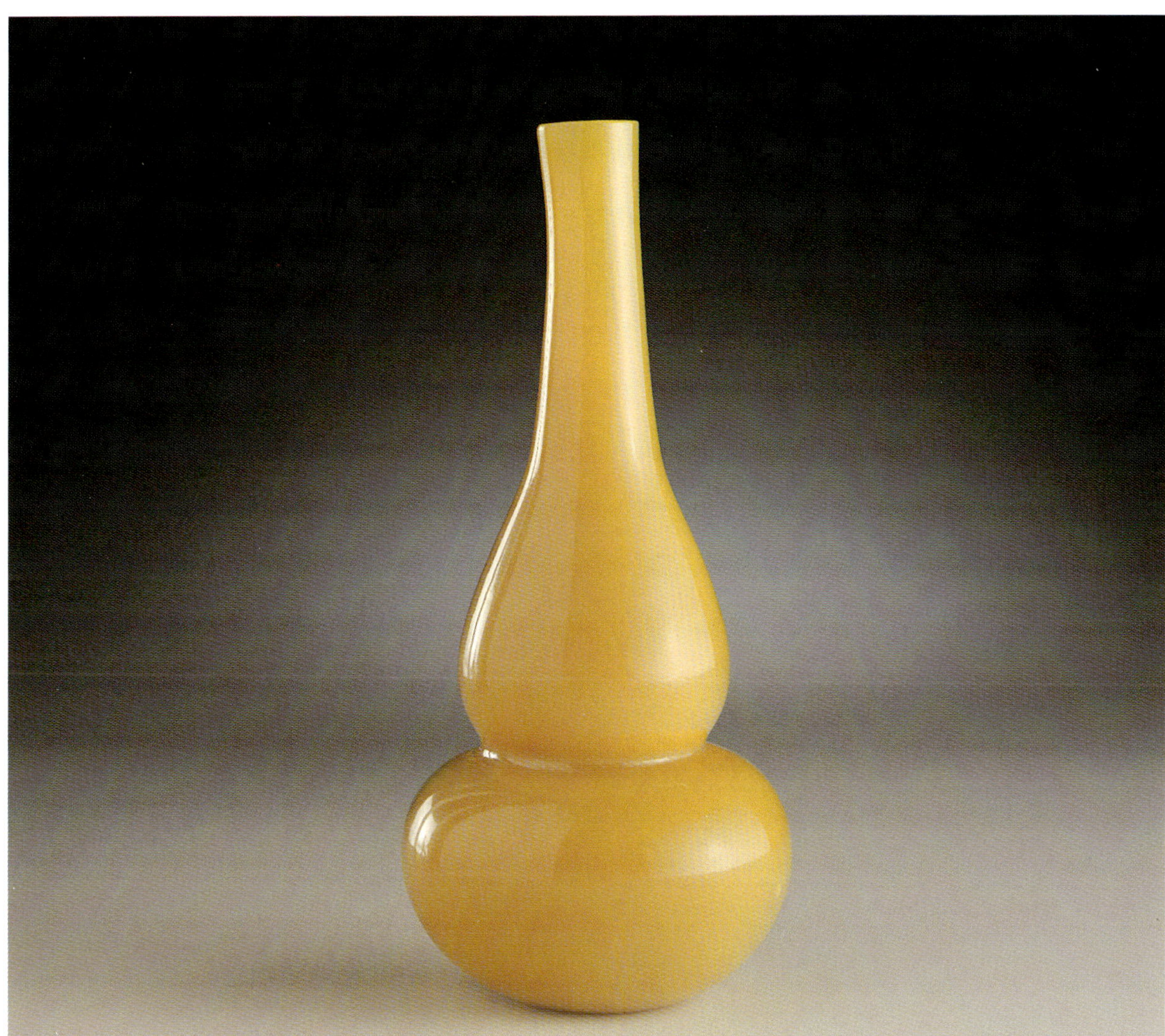

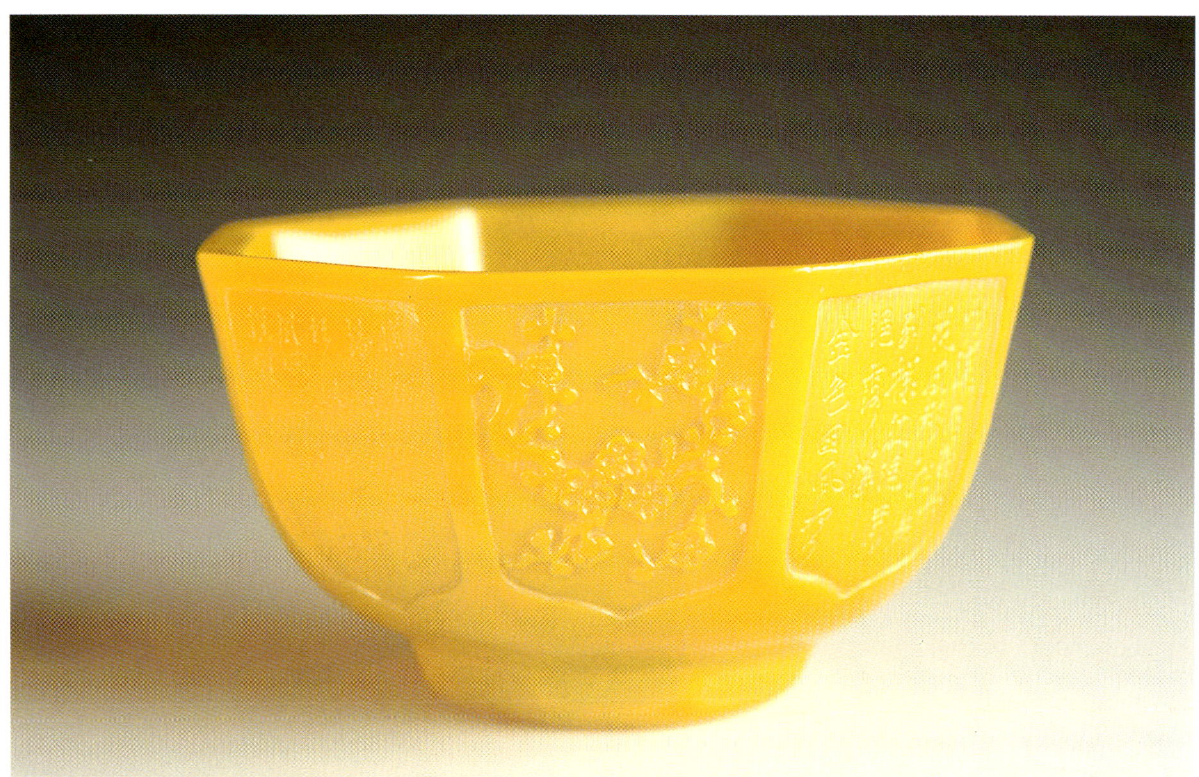

II

Octagonal bowl

Translucent yellow glass
Qing dynasty, Qianlong period, 1736-95
H: 11,9 cm

This **elegant octagonal bowl** has relatively thin walls that are slightly flared. Each of the eight sides has a large and deeply recessed shield shape panel. Four of the panels are incised in running script, each containing a different poem. The remaining four panels are delicately carved in relief with various flowers including prunus, magnolia and peony (one panel also depicts a bird). The quality of the carving is remarkably high with even small details such as the feathers of the bird and the veins on the flower petals carefully rendered. The bowl is supported on a high foot of octagonal shape with all the facets gently rounded. The hall mark **Cheng Xin Tang zhi** (made for the hall of complete trust) is finely incised in clerical script within a double square on the recessed base. The glass is of bright yellow color and is slightly opalescent. The yellow color is of fairly consistent tone throughout, except for the lower portion of the interior of the bowl which has some thin striations of darker yellow tone.

Technically and stylistically this piece is closely related to an octagonal bowl illustrated in Christie's, ***Fine Chinese Ceramics and Works of Art***, *New York, March 28, 1996, n° 93*, which has the mark **Qianlong nian zhi** incised on the base. The Christie's bowl is so similar in subject, technique and glass material that there seems to be little doubt that both are from the same workshop. This is an especially interesting point as the present piece includes a private hallmark (Cheng Xin Tang zhi). The high quality of the carving as well as the carving technique employed on both examples suggest the involvement of jade craftsmen or other lapidaries.

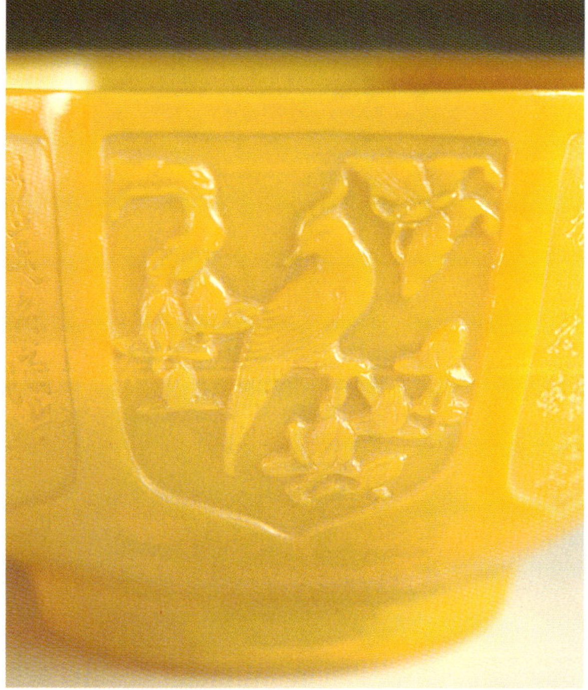

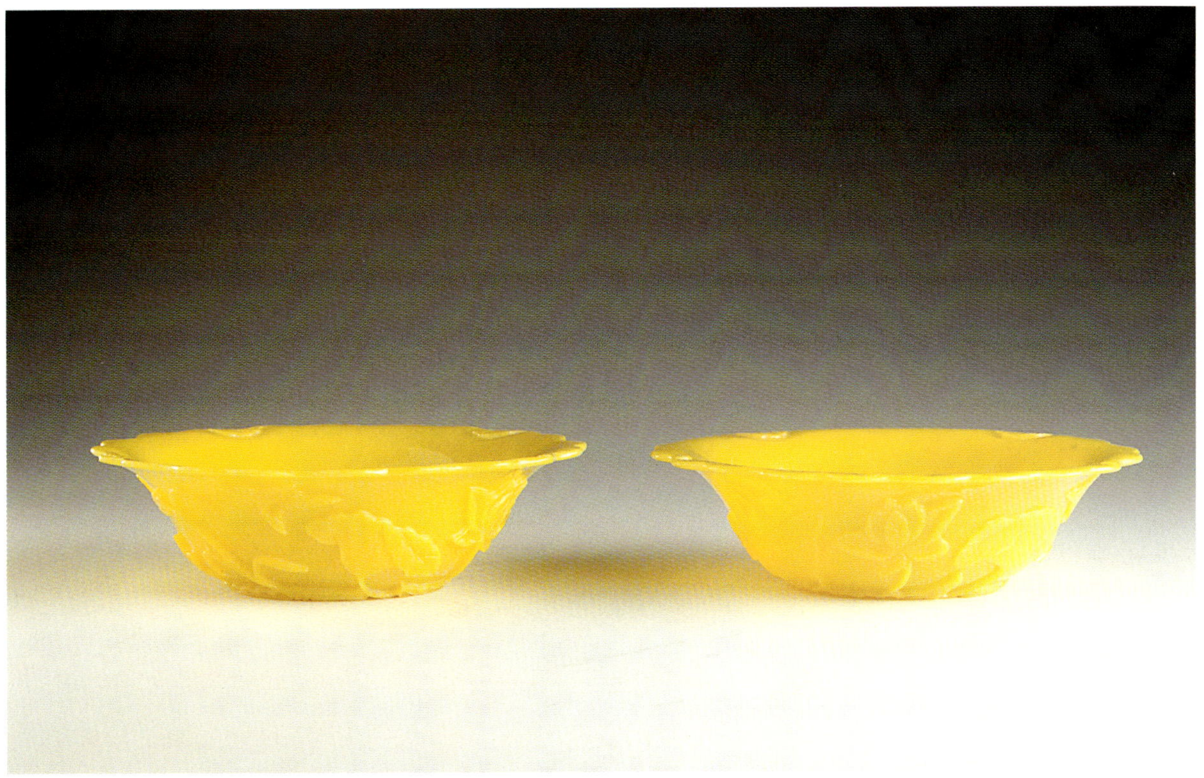

12

Pair of lotus leaf-shaped dishes

Carved opaque yellow glass
Qing dynasty, 18 th century
Diameter: 14,2 cm
Provenance: Yamanaka, Chicago

Each of the bowls in this pair is conceived as a large lotus leaf. The relatively thin, rounded walls rise steeply from the circular base and culminate in an everted, scalloped rim. The edge of five scallops on the exterior of the bowl and five on the interior are carved so as to resemble the folded edge of the lotus leaf. The exterior of each bowl is incised with thin lines to suggest the veins of the lotus leaf and is also carved in fairly high relief with a continuous design that features lotus leaves, lotus blossoms, stalks of millet as well as two egrets and a butterfly. The underside is naturalistically carved with two tied bundles of lotus stems and leaves, each of semi-circular shape. The base is slightly recessed and includes a carved stem of curled shape opposite a lotus pod supported on a gently bent stem. The glass is of opaque bright yellow color and is of consistent tone throughout both pieces.

Vessels shaped in a naturalistic form, especially as a lotus leaf, are not uncommon in Qing glass production. The present pair of bowls is, however, of exceptional quality. For related examples see cat.n° 27 in the present collection as well as *Clarence Shangraw and Claudia Brown,* ***A Chorus of Colors: Chinese Glass from Three American Collections****, exhibition catalogue, Asian Art Museum of San Francisco, 1995, page 123, cat. n° 100 from the collection of Mrs. Barney Dagen and page 124, cat. n° 101 from the collection of Alan E. Feen.*

Claudia Brown, in her commentary to the example in the collection of Mrs. Barney Dagen, notes that "the foliate bowl conceived as a lotus blossom has a long history in Chinese glass" and cites several Song and Yuan examples (*as cited page 123*). It should, however, be noted that most of the eighteenth and nineteenth century glass bowls are not actually conceived as a lotus blossom as were the earlier Song and Yuan glass examples, but rather as a lotus leaf.

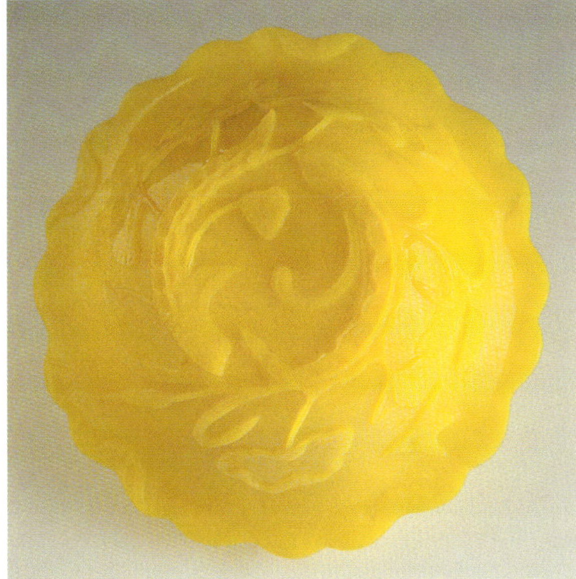

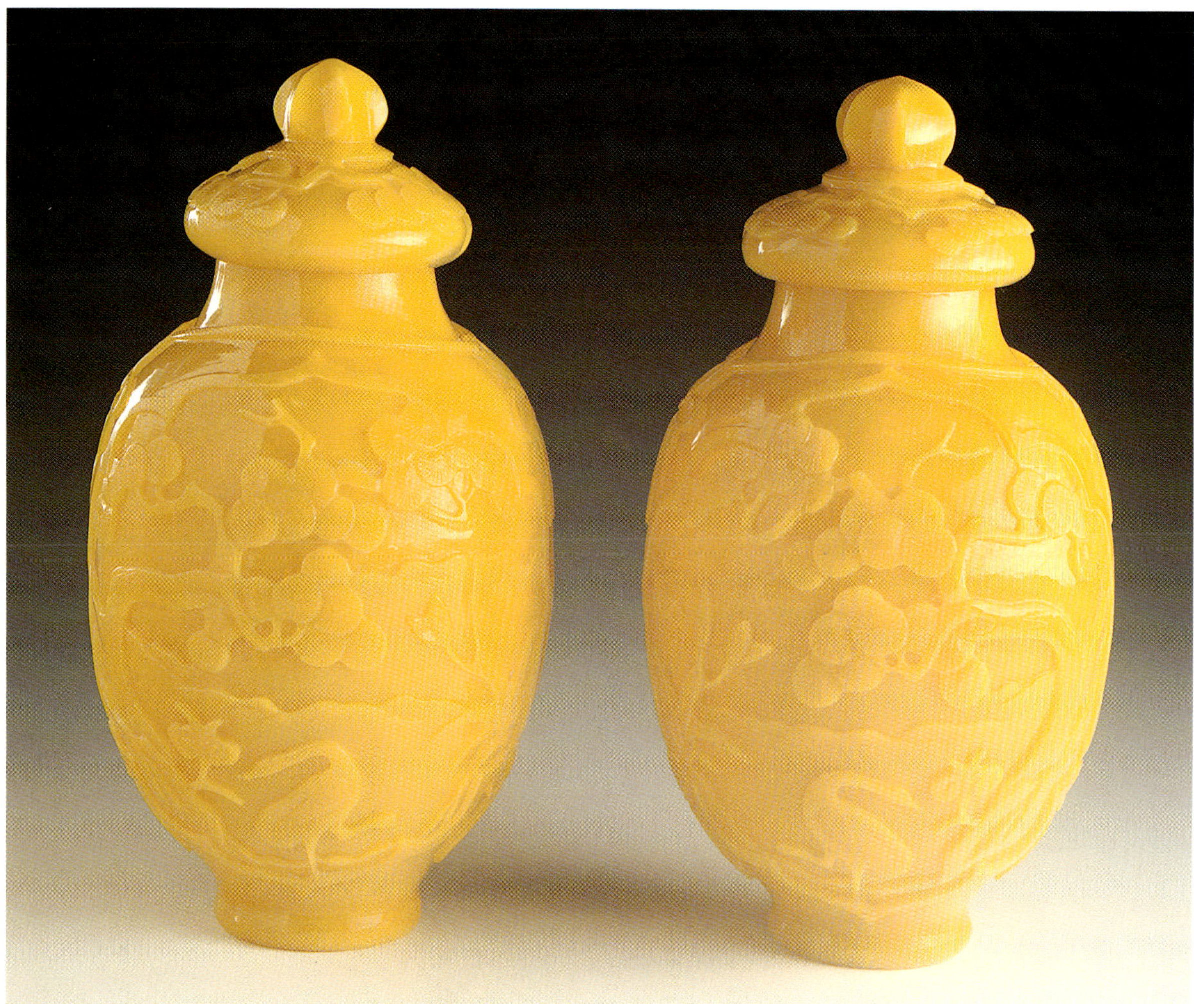

13

Pair of covered jars

Opaque yellow glass
Qing dynasty, 19 th century
H: 21,6 cm

This **pair of covered jars** each has a large ovoid body from which rises the broad, nearly cylindrical neck. The body is supported on a relatively small, short foot ring that surrounds a slightly recessed base. Both jars are carved in high relief with opposite matching designs contained in two cartouches, on one side the design features a deer and a pine tree and on the opposite side a crane, a **lingzhi** fungus and a pine tree. The base of the neck on each jar is carved so as to suggest that a thin cord is draped around it and that the cord's ends are tied into a loose bow that falls onto the narrow edges of the body. The lids are carved in relief with a pine tree motif. The fairly thick glass is of opaque yellow color and has a lustrous surface.

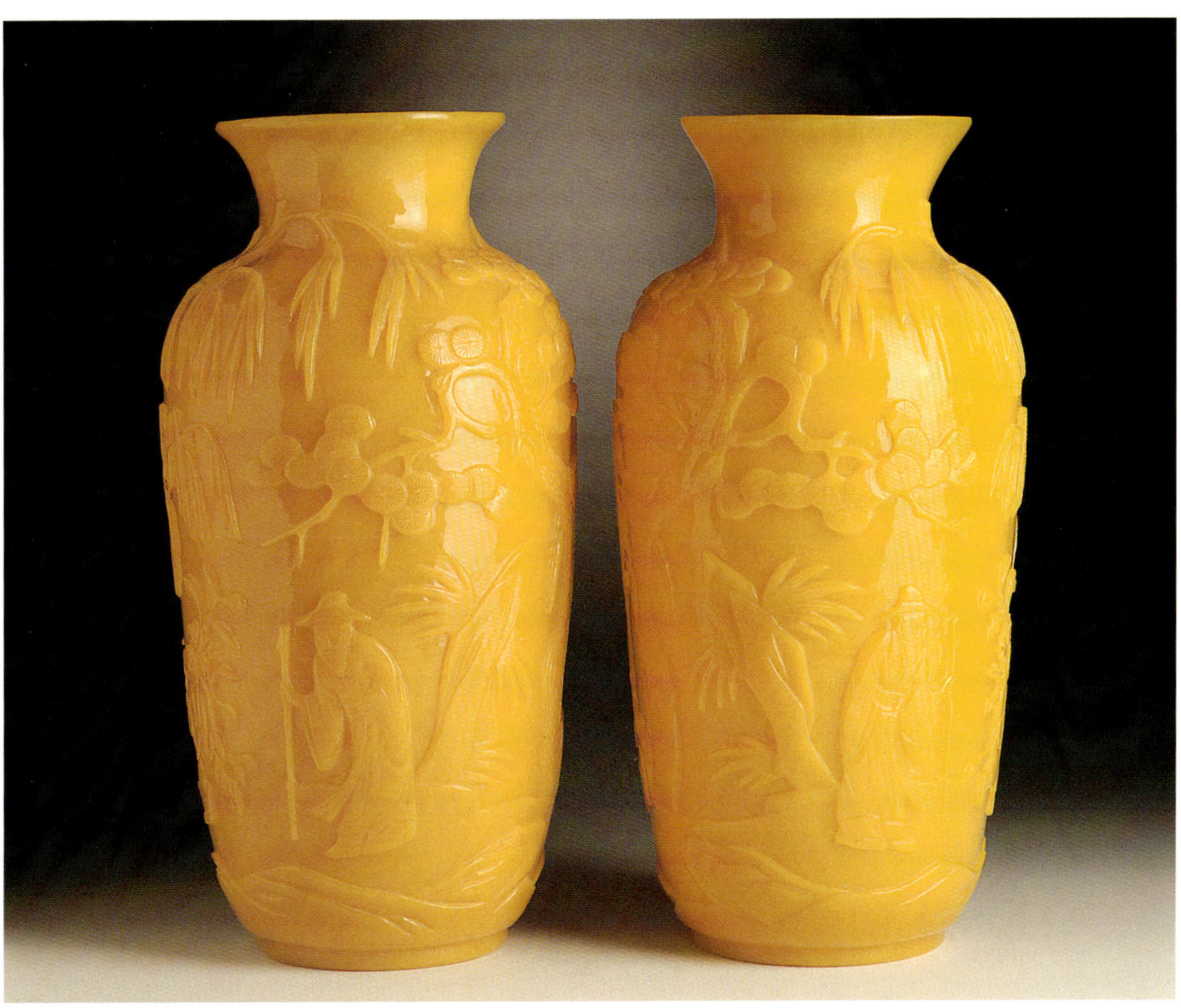

14

Pair of vases

Opaque yellow glass
Qing dynasty, 19 th century
H: 31,4 cm

This pair of imposing vases are carved in high relief in mirror image with a continuous landscape design that features several figures including the famous calligrapher Wang Hsi-chih (*ca. 303- ca. 361*) seated on a stone and gazing at a goose. The large cylindrical body of each vase tapers slightly toward the base and is supported on a relatively short foot ring that surrounds a slightly recessed base. The glass is of opaque bright yellow color and has some striations of lighter tone as well as small black inclusions throughout.

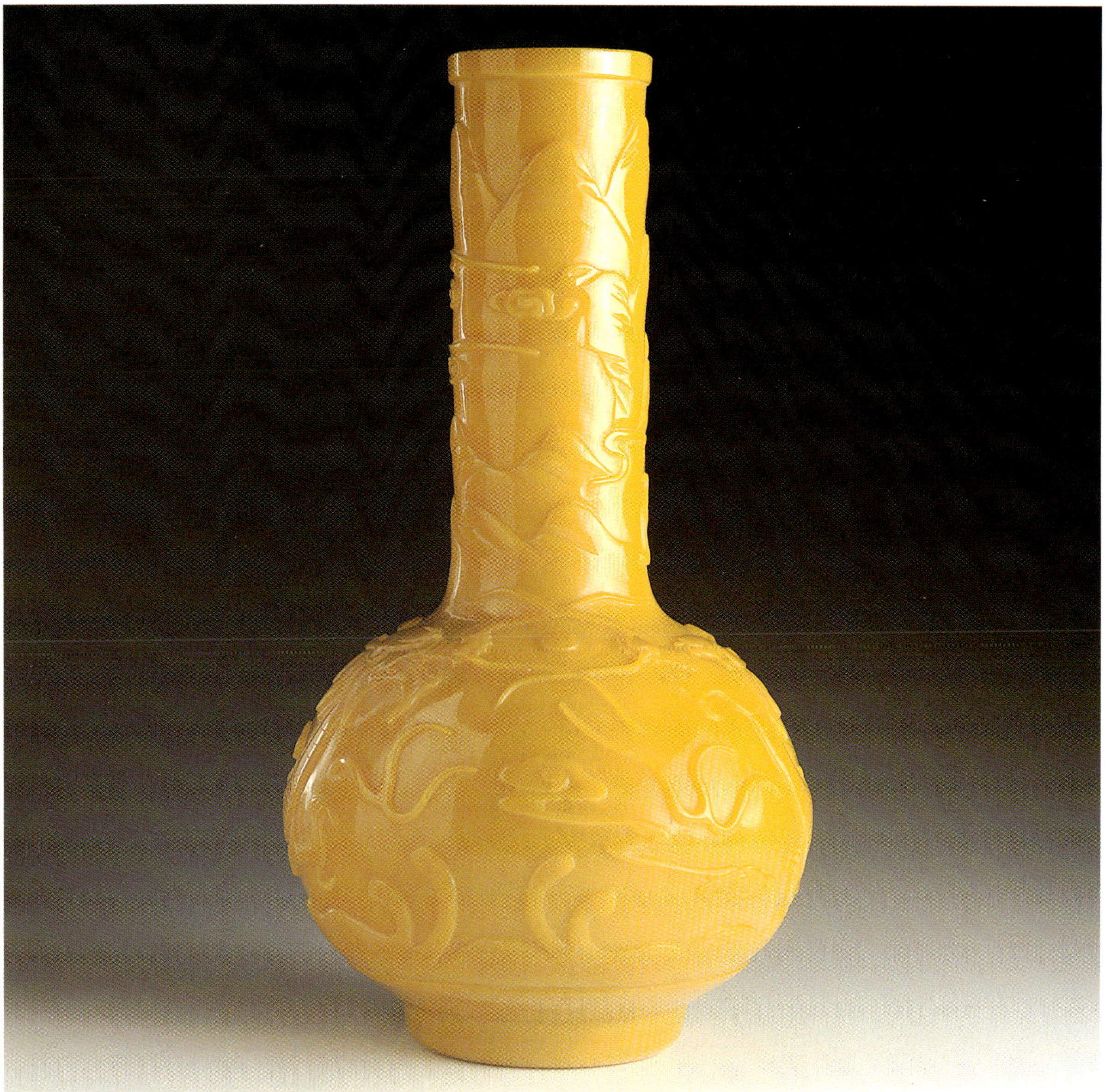

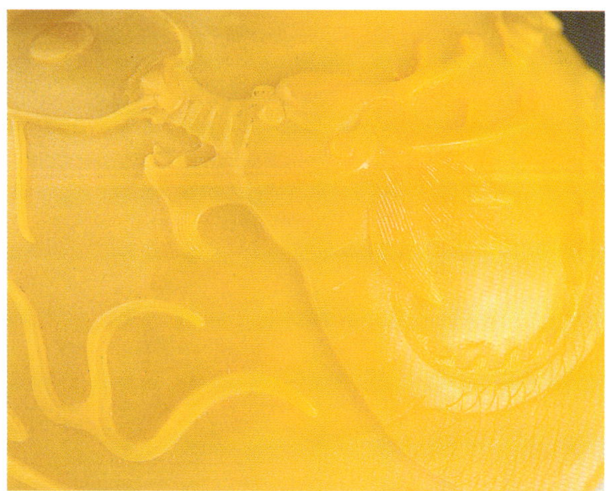

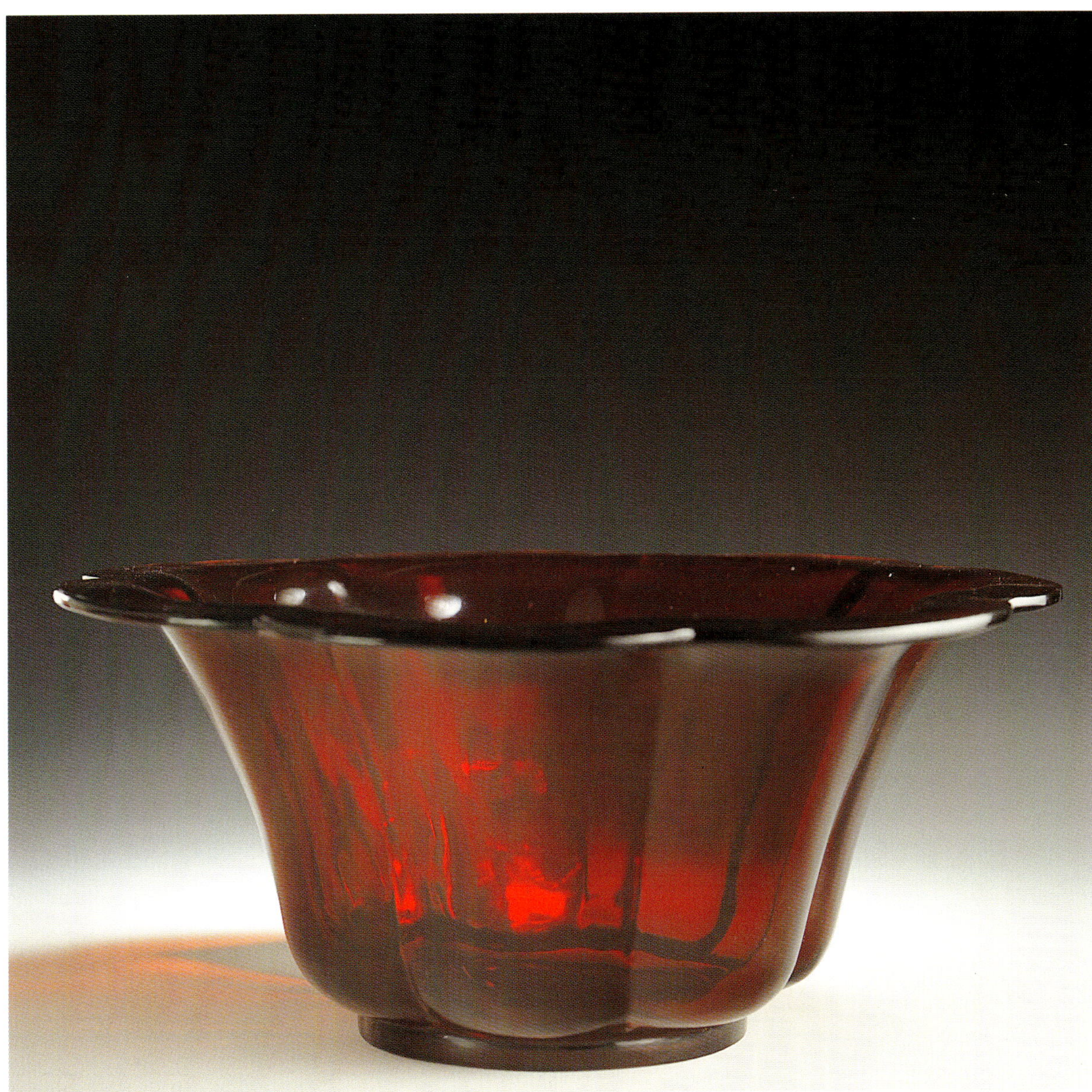

15

Large vase

Opaque yellow glass
Qing dynasty, Qianlong mark and period, 1736-95
H: 33,4 cm

The **bulbous body** and tall cylindrical neck of this impressive vase are finely carved in high relief with a continuous design that features two dragons confronting a pearl and also includes mountains and waves. The body is supported on a high foot ring that surrounds a slightly recessed base. The mark **Qianlong nian zhi** is incised in standard script within a double square on the base. The vase is well formed from a thick, opaque yellow glass that has numerous bubbles and inclusions. The color is fairly consistent throughout, but there is a relatively wide darker yellow striation directly above the foot ring where it connects to the undecorated band on the lower body.

16

Lobed bowl

Transparent red glass
Qing dynasty, Qianlong mark and period, 1736-95
H: 28,8 cm

This **massive seven-lobed bowl** has a wide everted rim and is supported on a high foot ring. The mark **Qianlong nian zhi** is incised in standard script within a bold square on the deeply recessed base and both the mark and the square retain traces of gold. The transparent red glass has numerous bubbles and inclusions as well as some minor crizzling on the upper portion of the interior surface.

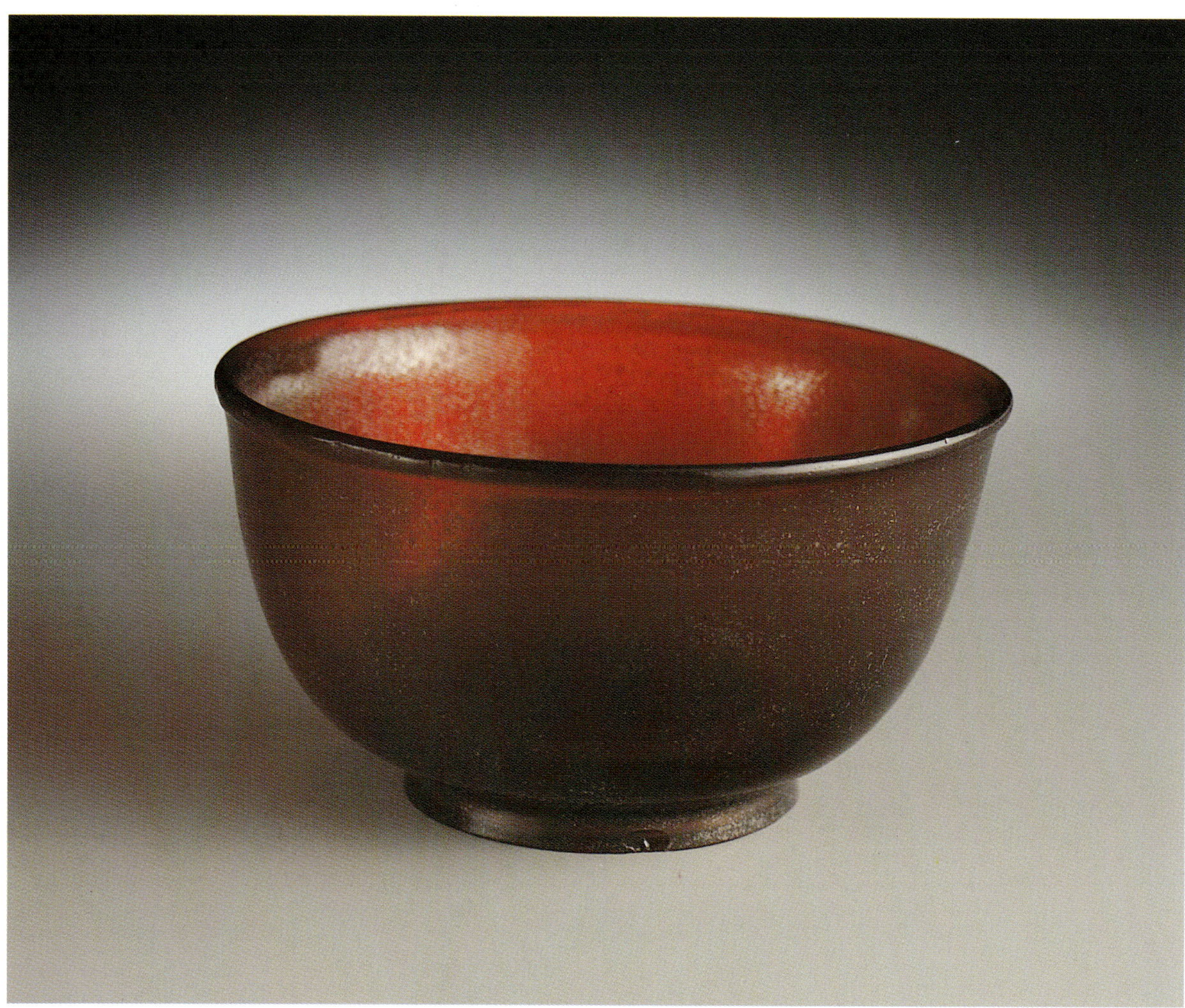

17

Bowl

Crizzled transparent red glass
Qing dynasty, Qianlong mark and period, 1736-95
H: 10,8 cm

This **beautifully formed bowl** has rounded, gently flared walls that ascend to a thin, rolled rim. The transparent deep red glass is extensively crizzled on both its inner and outer surfaces. The bowl is supported on a high, slightly flared foot ring that also bears considerable crizzling. Only the deeply recessed base, on which the mark **Qianlong nian zhi** is finely incised in standard script within a double square, is entirely free of crizzling. In spite of its relatively small size this bowl is extremely heavy.

Transparent red glass was successfully produced in the Qing dynasty as early as the Kangxi period. Even though no piece of transparent red glass is known to have survived from this period, visual evidence can be found to support this in a court painting of a lady reading a book from the set of **Twelve Beauties in the Yuanmingyuan** which dates to the Kangxi period and is in the collection of the Palace Museum in Beijing (see *Tian Jiaqing, "**Early Qing Furniture in a Set of Qing Dynasty Court Painting**". in Orientations, January 1993, volume 24, n° 1, page 32, fig. 2*). This painting includes a red glass snuff bottle on the table on which the lady rests her arm.

The extensive crizzling seen on this Qianlong mark and period bowl is most likely a consequence of the development and experimentation with different formulas for transparent red glass rather than the result of an unsuccessful new glass color.

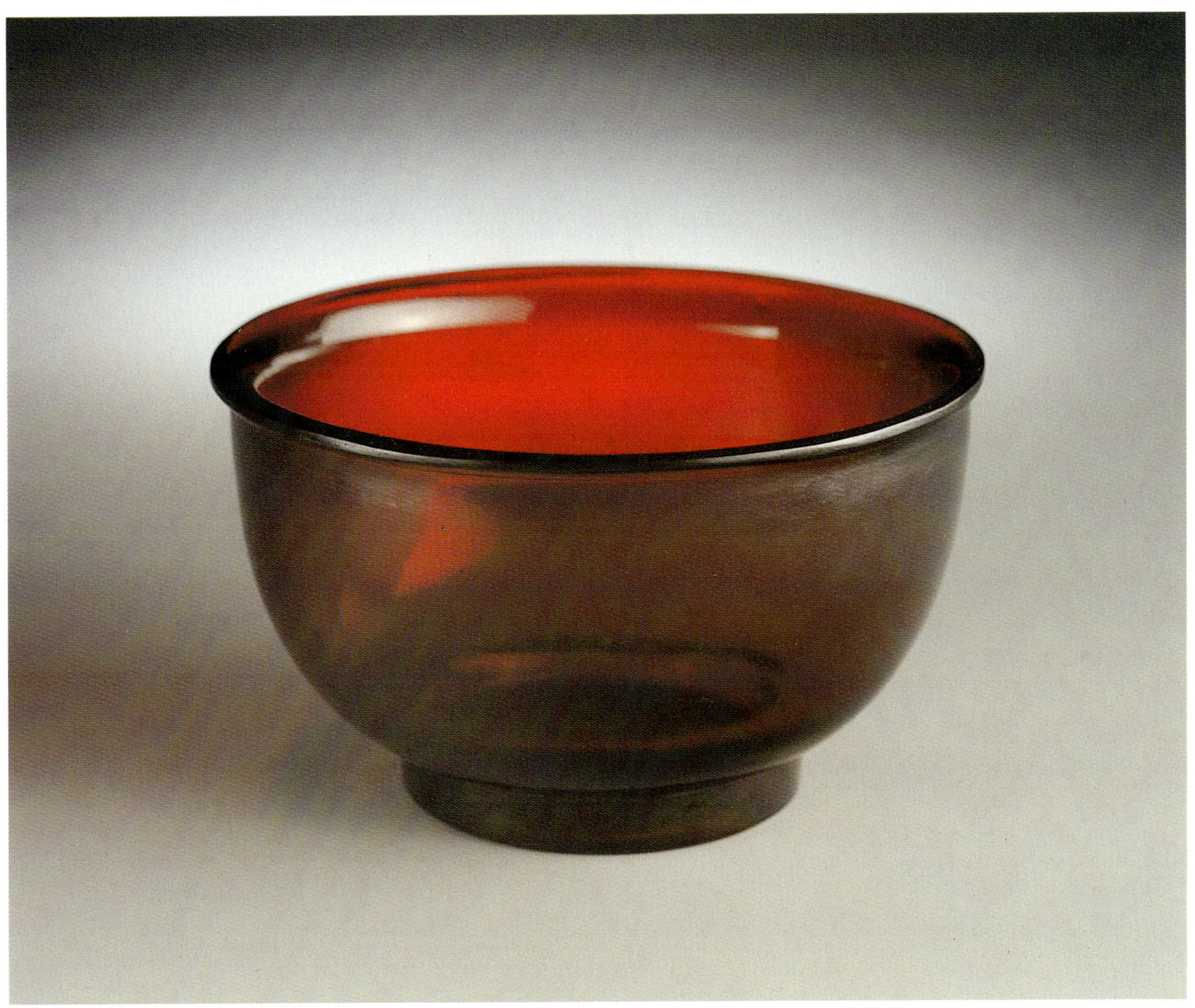

18

Bowl

Transparent red glass
Qing dynasty, 18 th century
H: 11 cm

T**his well formed u-shape bowl** has a thick, rolled rim. A shallow depression in the interior corresponds to the form of the base. The bowl is supported on a high foot ring that surrounds a fairly deep recessed base. The transparent red glass has a metallic-like luster and numerous small bubbles. Even though the bowl is larger than the previous example (*n° 17*) it is of a significantly lighter weight.

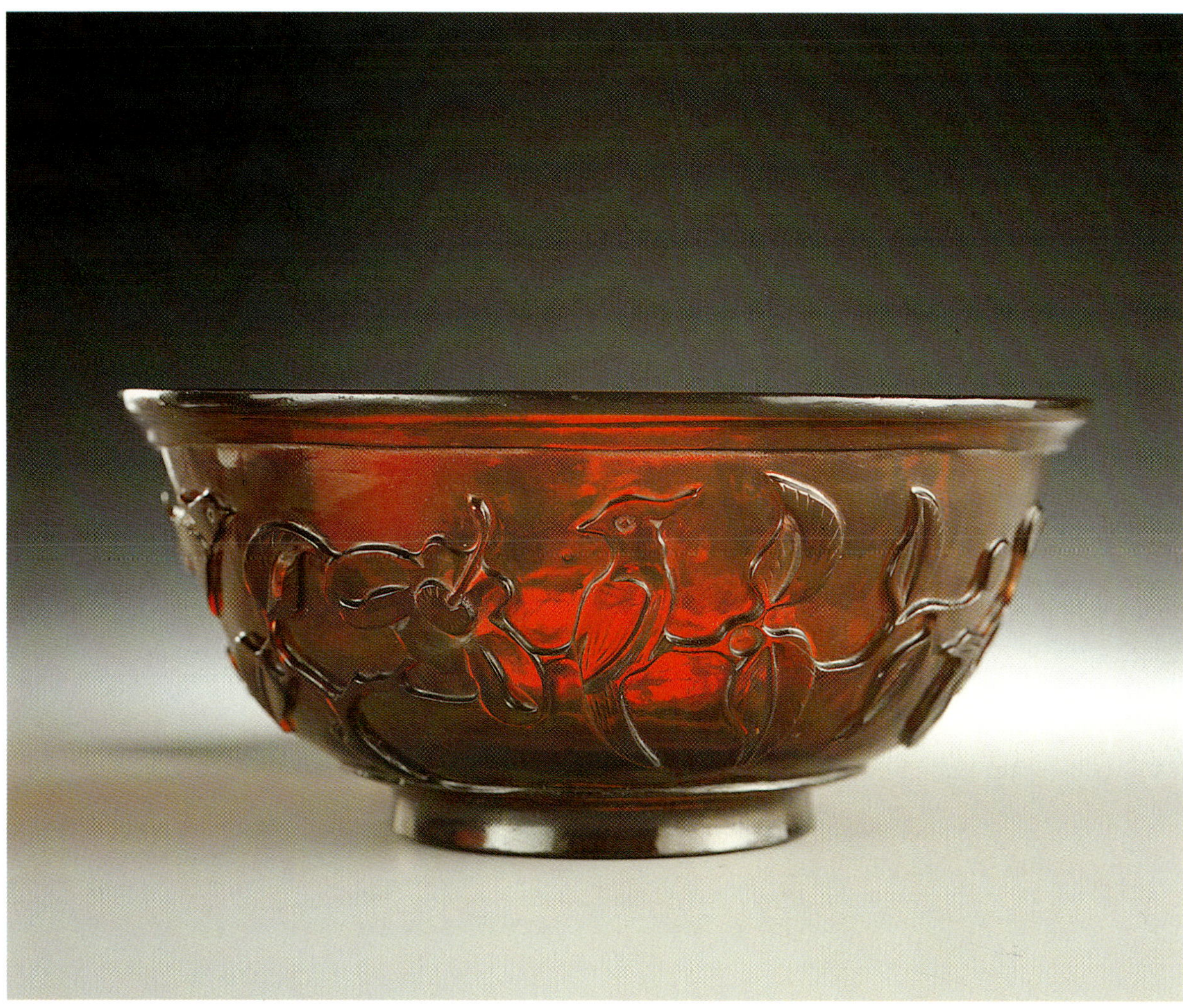

19

Bowl

Transparent red glass
Qing dynasty, 18 th - 19 th century
H: 16 cm

This **bowl** has rounded, gently flared walls that culminate in a thin, everted rim. The exterior is carved in fairly high relief with a continuous design of various flowers and birds that are contained within a wide band. The bowl is supported on a high foot ring that surrounds a deeply recessed base. The transparent ruby red glass is of a strong, consistent color and has only a few scattered bubbles.

20

Vase of *meiping* shape

Opaque pink glass
Qing dynasty, 18 th century
H: 15,2 cm

This **graceful *meiping*-shape** vase has well proportioned, bulging shoulders that curve inward and ascend to a short, gently flared neck. The circular base is flat. The glass is of opaque pink color with some striations of lighter tone as well as small bubbles throughout.

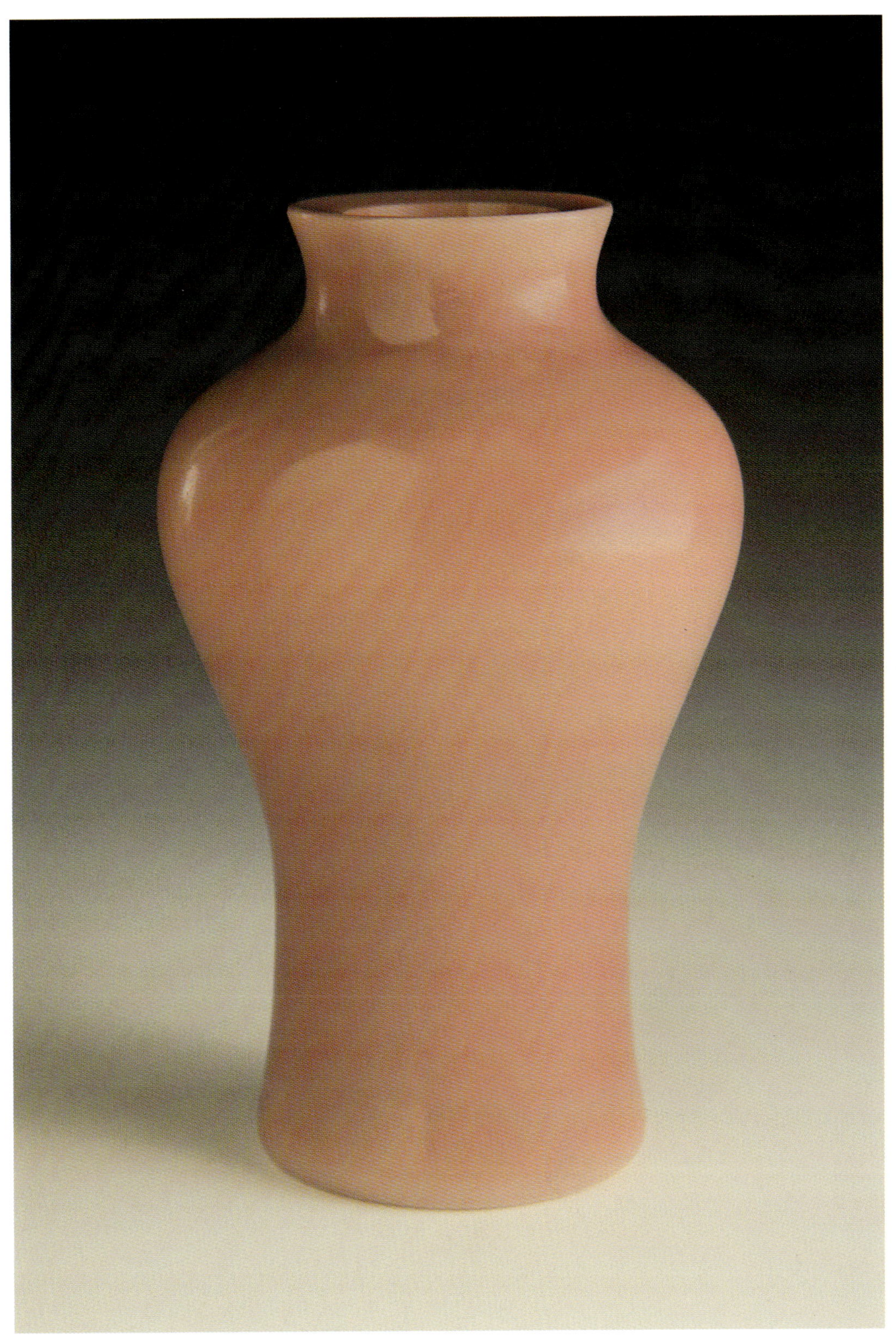

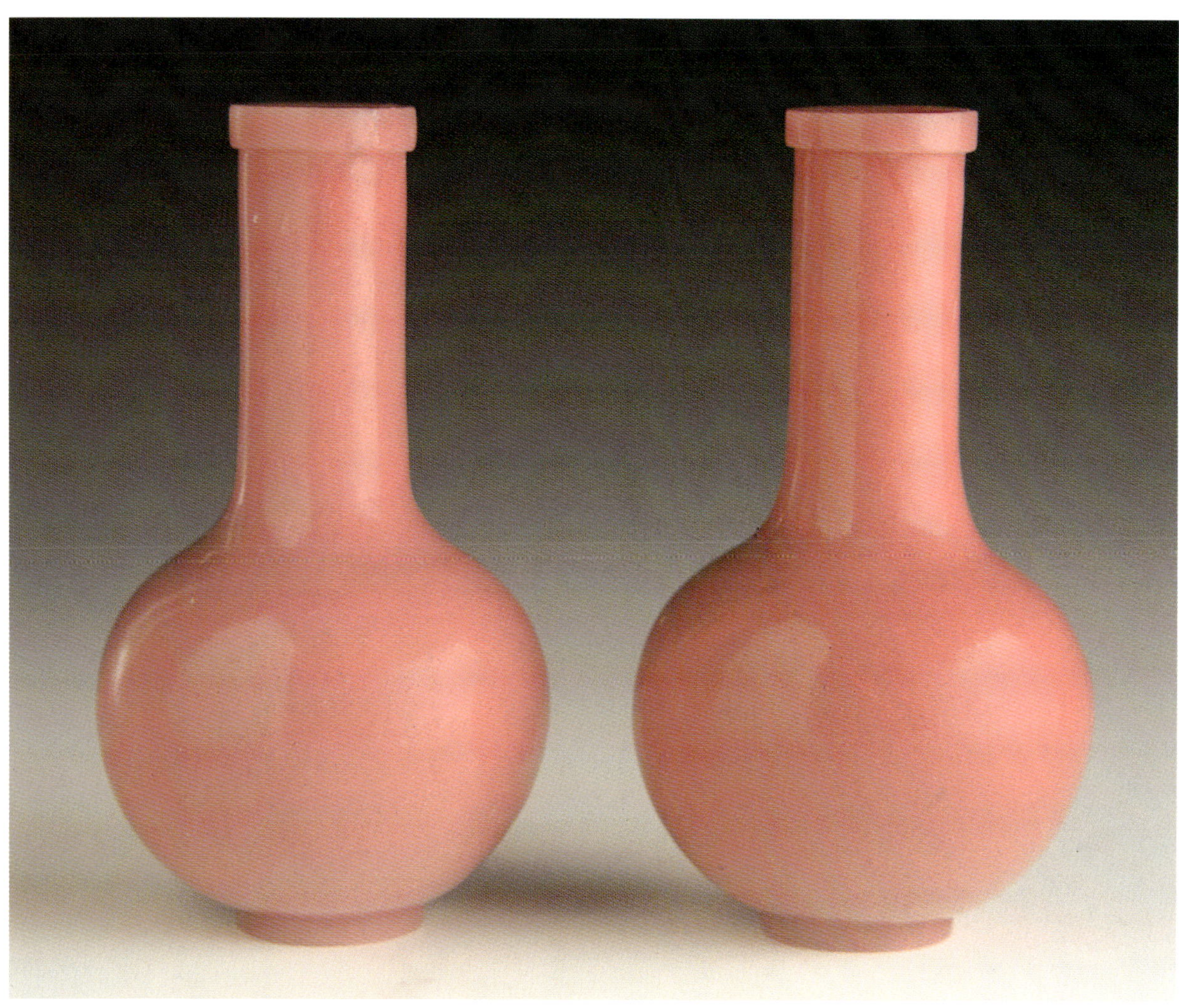

21

Pair of small vases

Opaque pink glass
Qing dynasty, 18 th - 19 th century
H: 11 cm

In this pair each vase has a globular body from which rises the tall, nearly cylindrical neck with a very wide rim. The body is supported on a small, short foot ring that surrounds a slightly recessed base. Both vases are formed from a relatively thick glass of opaque pink color that has some bubbles and inclusions throughout.

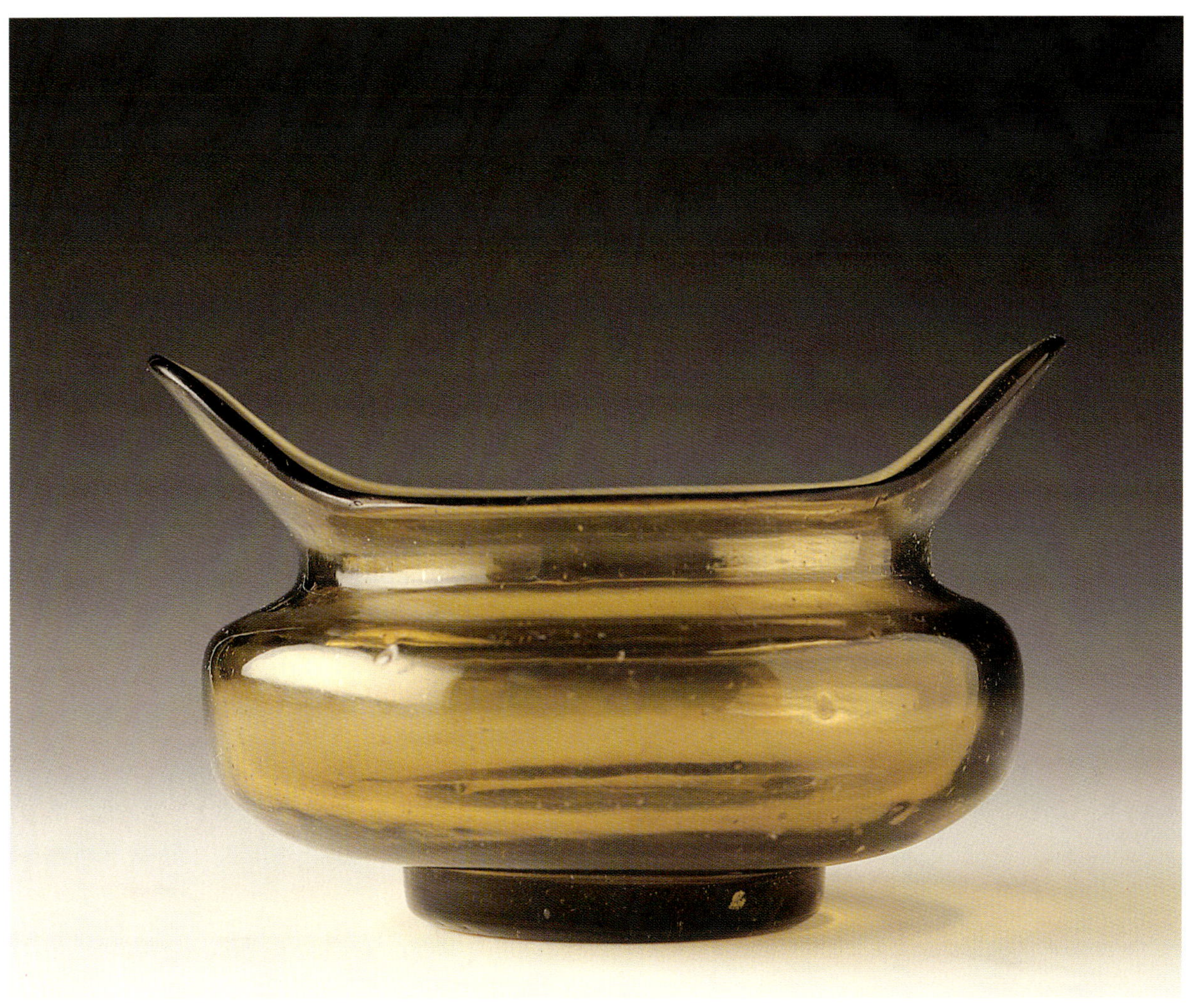

22

Censer

Transparent yellow-green glass
Qing dynasty, Guangxu mark and period, 1875-1908
H: 5,7 cm

This stout incense burner has a slightly asymmetrical compressed bulbous body. The relatively short cylindrical neck has two large oval shape handles with solid, gently bowed walls that flare sharply outward. The body is supported on a high foot ring. The mark **Guangxu nian zhi** is incised in standard script within a double square on the flat base. The glass is of transparent yellow-green color and is suffused with bubbles.

23

Large vase

Transparent peacock-blue glass
Qing dynasty, Qianlong mark and period, 1736-95
H: 25,8 cm

Transparent, vivid peacock-blue vase with only a few scattered inclusions and bubbles, the glass of this bottle vase has a jewel-like brilliance. An internal crack is visible on one side of the lower body and may have developed in the production of the piece. The nearly cylindrical neck raises above the very full, bulbous body supported on a high foot ring. The mark **Qianlong nian zhi** is incised in standard script within a large square on the slightly recessed base.

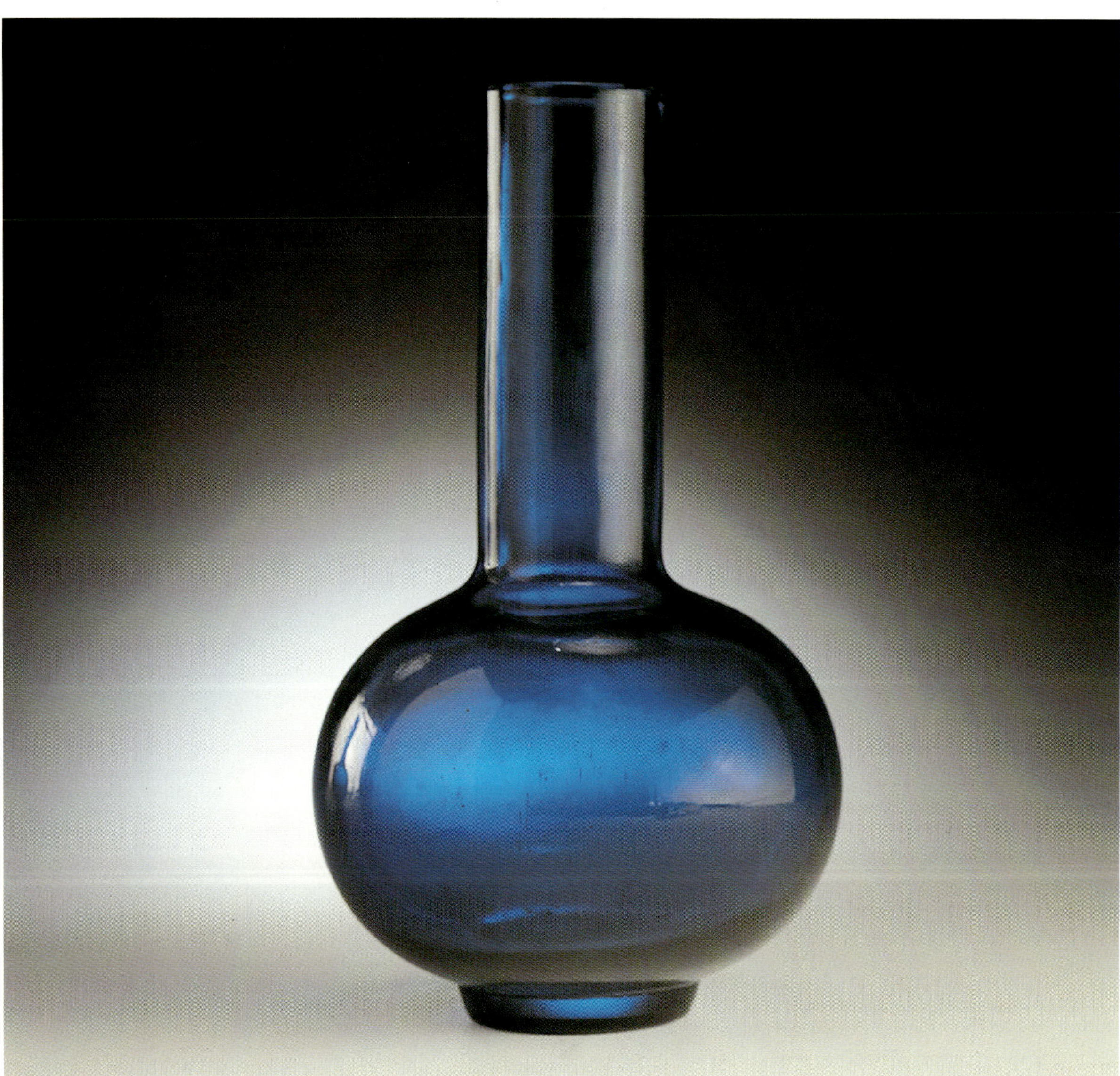

24

Large vase

Transparent peacock-blue glass
Qing dynasty, Qianlong mark and period, 1736-95
H: 24,9 cm

This vase forms a matched pair with the previous example (*no. 23*). The glass is of slightly darker peacock-blue color on this vase than on the other one and has a greater number of bubbles and inclusions, including a relatively large inclusion of salt-like appearance on the midsection of the neck. The cylindrical neck is not as wide on this example as on the previous one and is gently flared. The bulbous body is supported on a high foot ring that tapers toward the base. The mark **Qianlong nian zhi** is incised in standard script within a double square on the deeply recessed base. Although this vase is slightly smaller than the previous one it is significantly heavier.

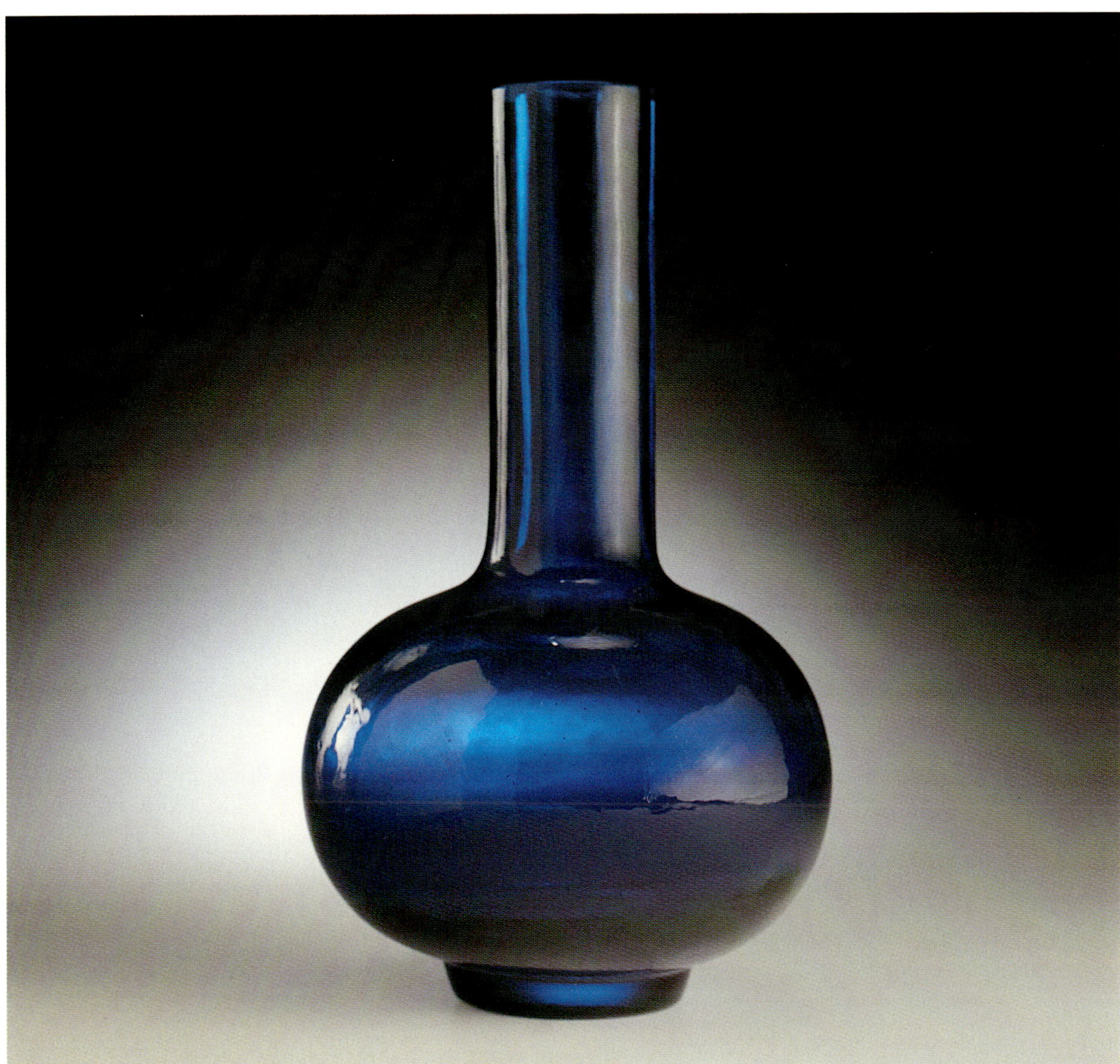

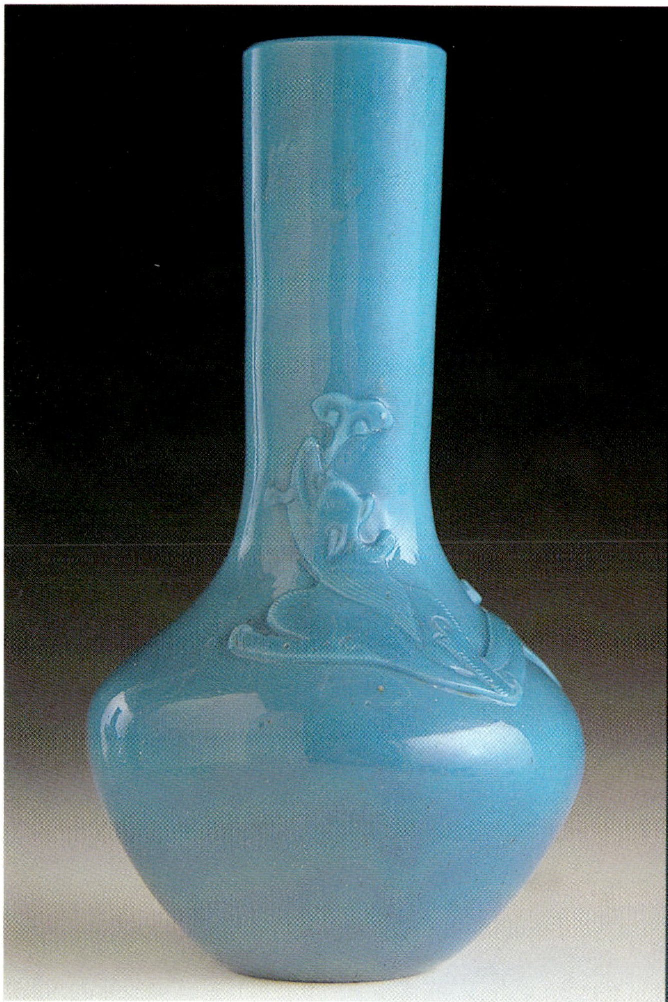

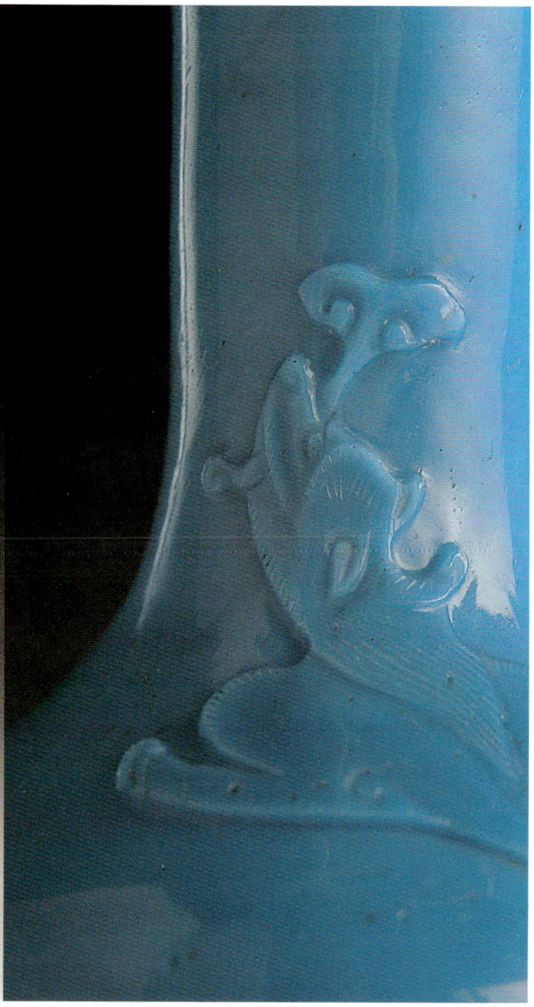

25

Vase

Opaque bright blue glass possibly imitating turquoise
Qing dynasty, Qianlong mark and period, 1736-95
H: 17,1 cm

Lacking a foot ring, the thick walls of this attractive vase spring directly from the base, rise steeply, and then curve inward at the shoulder. The long, nearly cylindrical neck flares slightly toward the rim. Finely carved in low relief, primarily on the upper portion of the compressed bulbous body, is a **zhilong** that holds a piece of **lingzhi** fungus in its mouth and has its head raised upward toward the neck of the vase. The mark **Qianlong nian zhi** is incised in standard script within a double square on the deeply recessed base. The glass is of opaque bright blue color that has some thin striations of darker tone and resembles the mineral turquoise. There is some pitting visible on the exterior surface as well as a small area of crizzling near the base.

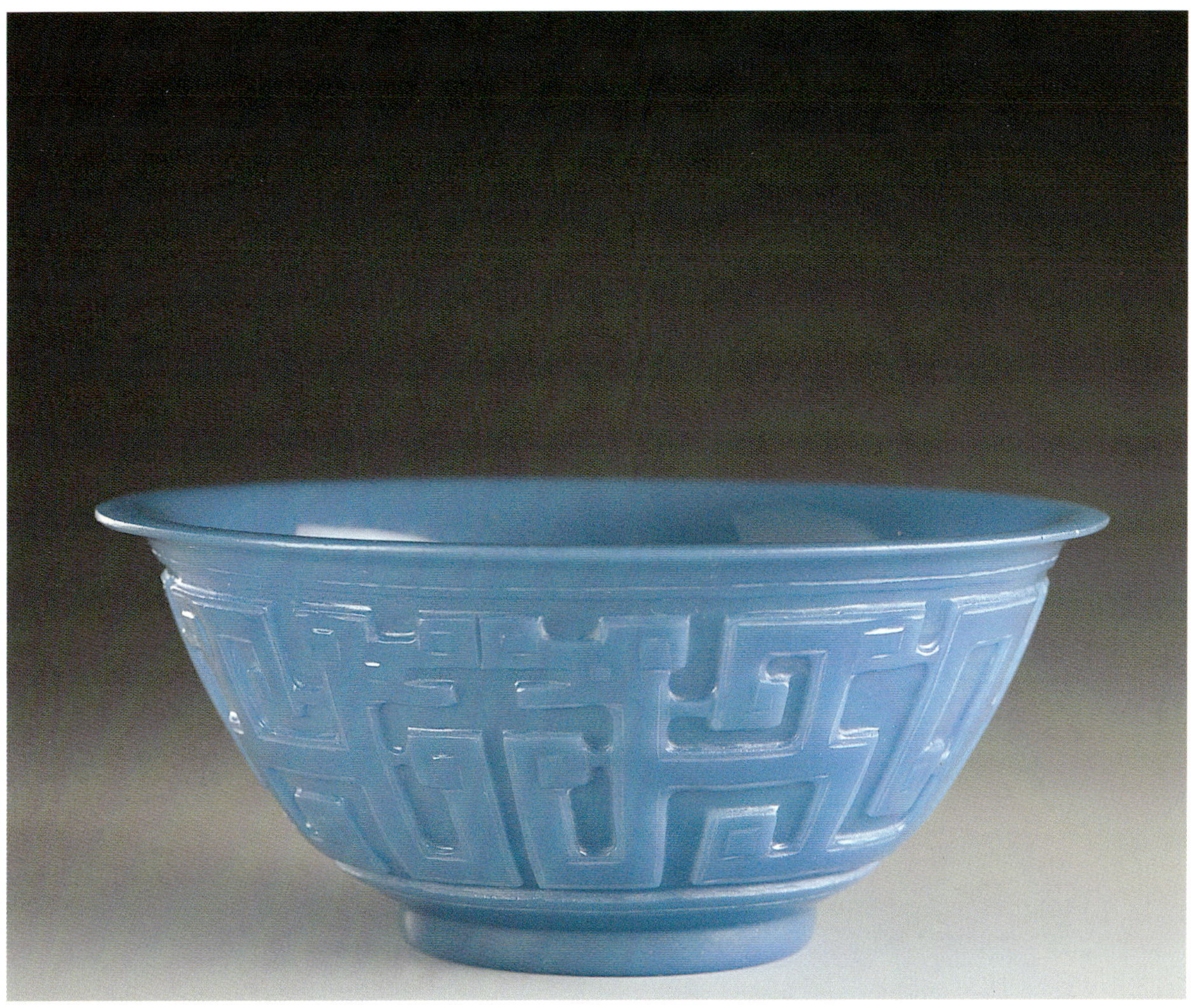

26

Bowl

Translucent violet-blue glass
Qing dynasty, 19 th century
Diam: 17,1 cm

This deep bowl has rounded, gently flared walls that culminate in an everted rim. A single wide band encircles the exterior and encloses a carved archaistic pattern of squared spirals with dragons heads. The edges of the squared spirals are incised with a thin line so as to enhance the three dimensional quality of the strongly linear design. The bowl is supported on a fairly high foot ring that surrounds a slightly recessed base. The thin glass is of unusual, translucent violet-blue color.

A pair of jars formed from glass of nearly identical color are in the collection from Mrs. Barney Dagen; see *Clarence Shangraw and Claudia Brown,* ***A Chorus of Colors: Chinese Glass from Three American Collections****, exhibition catalogue, Asian Art Museum of San Francisco, 1995, page 125, cat. n° 102.*

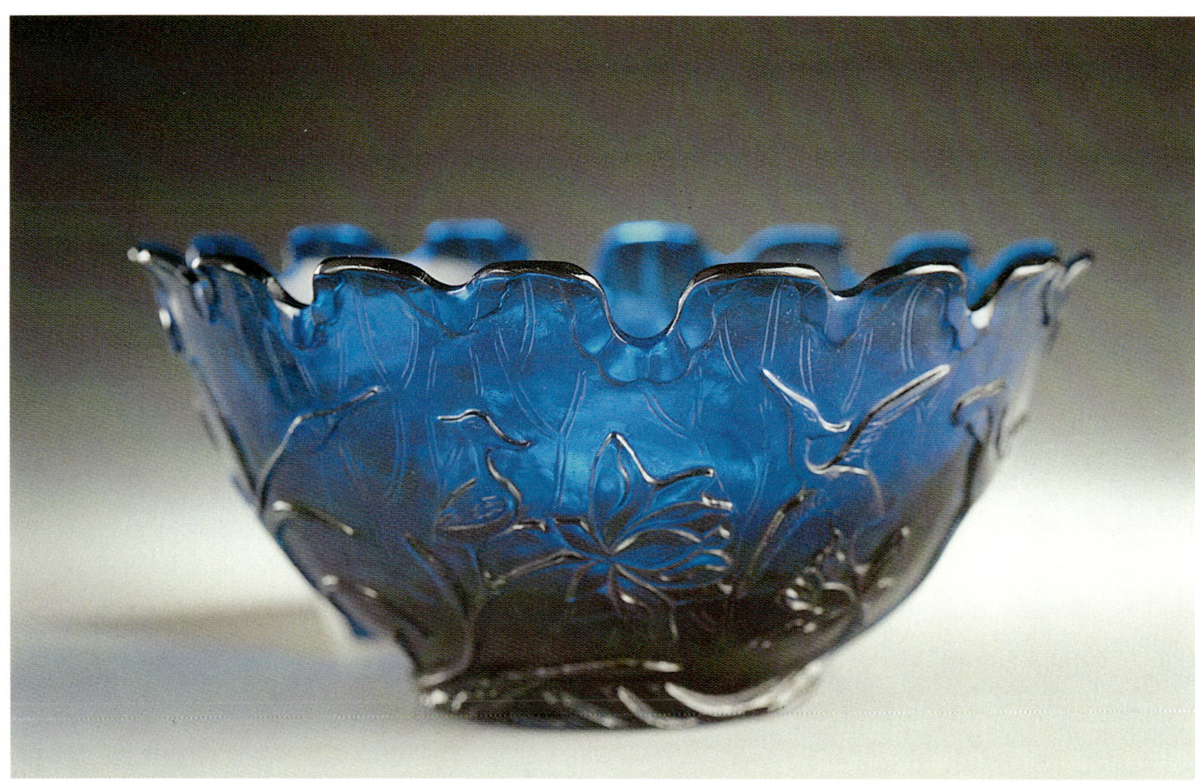

27

Lotus leaf-shaped bowl

Transparent blue glass
Qing dynasty, 19 th century
Diam: 16,4 cm

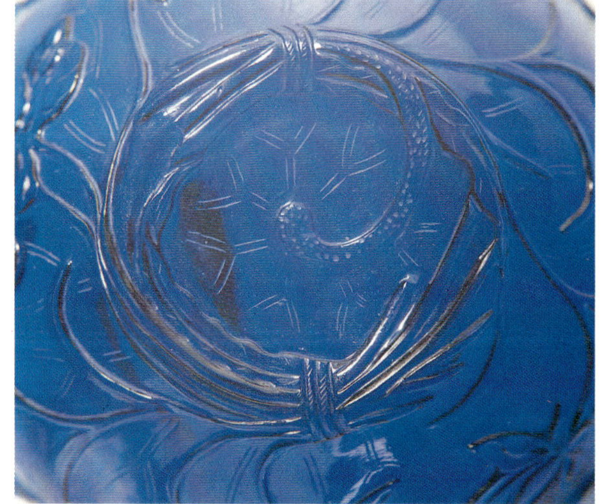

This **bowl** is conceived as a large lotus leaf. It has thin, rounded walls that are gently flared and culminate in a scalloped rim. The rim has an unusually large number of scallops, eight large alternating with eight of smaller size. The exterior of each scallop is carved so as to resemble the folded over edge of the lotus leaf. The exterior of the body is incised with thin lines to suggest the veins of the lotus leaf and is also carved in fairly high relief with a continuous design that features lotus blossoms, leaves and pods as well as three egrets. The bowl is supported on a relatively high foot ring that is naturalistically carved on the exterior as well as on the underside as two tied bundles of lotus stems and leaves. The center of the slightly recessed base is carved with the curled stem of the lotus leaf. The glass is of transparent blue color and is of consistent tone throughout the piece.

28

Vase

Transparent deep blue glass
Qing dynasty, 19 th century
Diam: 24,1 cm

This vase has a large bulbous body from which rises the tall, nearly cylindrical neck with a wide rim. The body is encircled by a very high relief with a design that features various types of fruit and also includes several butterflies. The upper portion of the neck are with long, stylized leaves and the base of the neck is encircled by a wide band incised with a continuous weave-like pattern. The body tapers dramatically toward the base and forms a high foot ring which is enclosed by carved upright leaves. The base is slightly recessed. The glass is of transparent deep blue, almost purple, color.

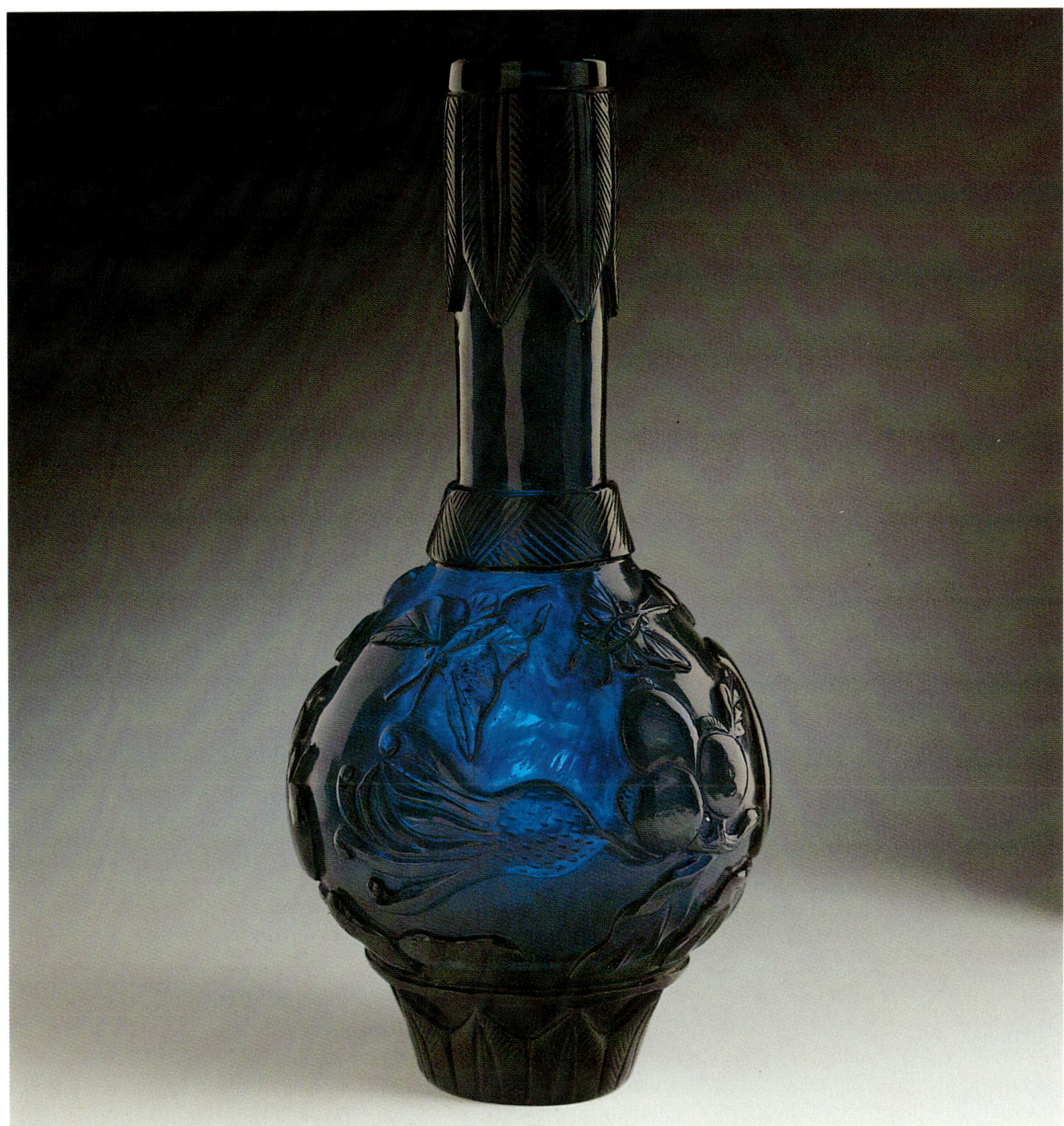

29

Massive bowl

Transparent purple glass
Qing dynasty, Qianlong mark and period, 1736-95
Diam: 29,8 cm
Provenance: Kerteum, Buenos Aires

This **impressive bowl** has fairly thin walls that expand outward, then gently rise and culminate in a thickened rim. The exterior is carved in high relief with a continuous design of military action. Included in the scene are two footmen each carrying a large banner. On one banner is incised the character **shuai** (general) and on the other is incised the character **hou** (probably the rank or possibly the family name of the nearby warrior). The bowl is supported on a high foot ring that surrounds a slightly recessed base. The mark **Qianlong nian zhi** is incised in standard script within a bold square on the base. The glass is of transparent deep purple color and is of consistent tone throughout the large piece.

The scene of military action on this unusually large bowl is similar to that which appears on the lower portion of the well-known red overlay vase in the collection of the Corning Museum of Glass (see, *Robert J. Charleston*, ***Masterpieces of Glass: A World History from the Corning Museum of Glass***, *New York, 1980, page 181, n° 82*) and also illustrated in *Claudia Brown and Donald Rabiner*, **Clear as Crystal, Red as Flame: Later Chinese Glass**, *exhibition catalogue, New York, China House Gallery, China Institute of America, 1990, page 83, cat. n° 49.*

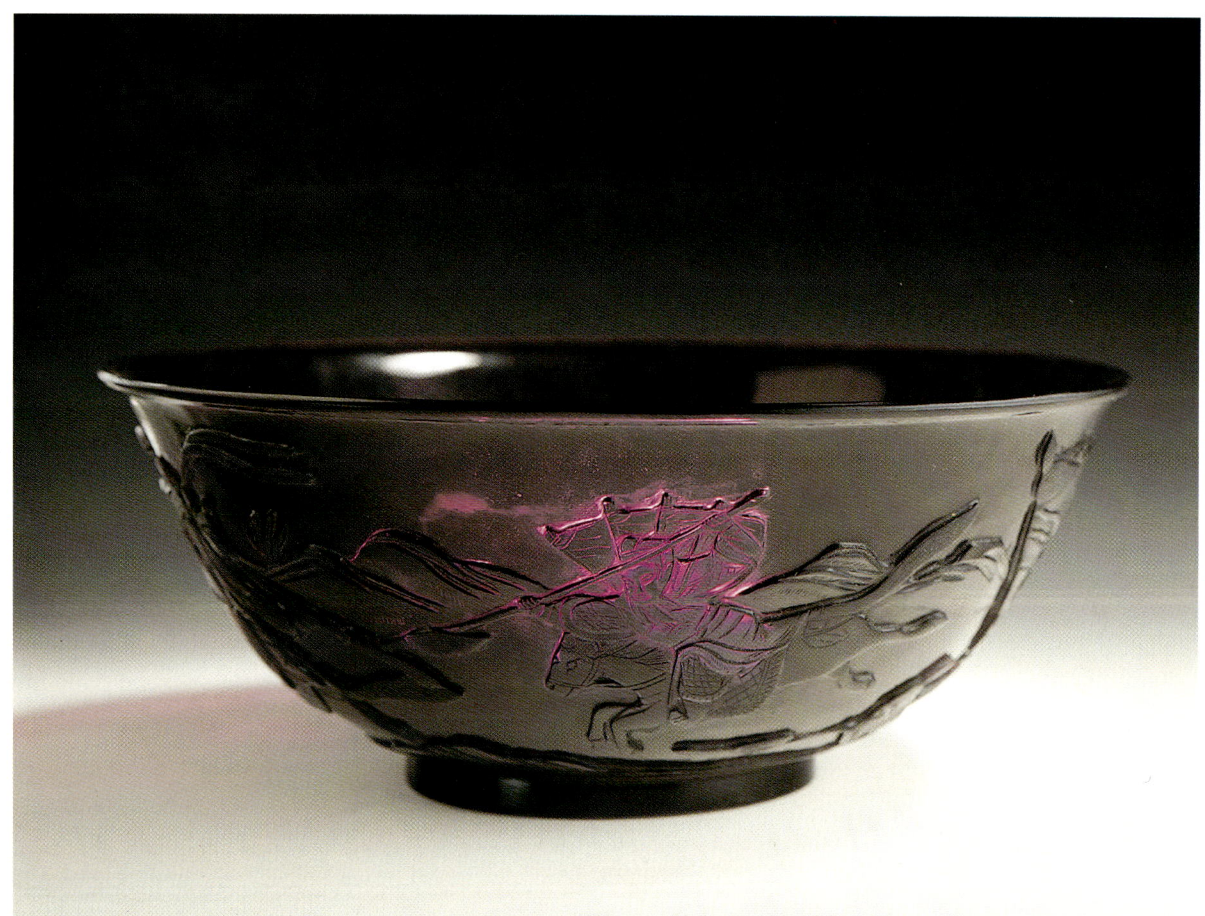

30

Tripod vessel

Crizzled opaque brown glass
Qing dynasty, Yongzheng mark and period, 1723-35
Diam: 8,1 cm
Published: Spink and Son Ltd., Chinese Jewellery, Accessories and Glass, *London, 1991, page 57, n°102*

This well formed tripod vessel has a sturdy, compressed bulbous body with small, gently rounded shoulders. The short cylindrical neck is slightly flared and culminates in a thickened rim. The body is supported on three evenly spaced legs that are each formed as an abstract animal leg. The mark **Yongzheng nian zhi** is incised in standard script on the rounded base of the body. The glass is of opaque brown color with some thin striations of darker tone primarily on the lower portion of the body where there is also some crizzling. The surface is smooth and lustrous.

The exact function of this rare Yongzheng mark and period tripod vessel is not easy to determine. It has previously been identified as a censer (*see Spink and Son, Ltd. as cited above and also Christie's,* ***Fine Chinese Ceramics, Jades and Works of Art****, New York, November 29, 1990, n° 95*). There is, however, a second possibility that in the Yongzheng period this form was intended to be used as a brush washer. Palace archives record that during the Yongzheng period three-legged opaque white and red overlay brush washers were made at the Yuanming Yuan summer palace (*see Yang Boda, "A Brief Account of Qing Dynasty Glass" in Claudia Brown and Donald Rabiner,* ***Chinese Glass of the Qing Dynasty, 1644-1911: The Robert H. Clague Collection****, exhibition catalogue, Phoenix Art museum, 1987, page 78*).

Even though the exact function of this particular form remains uncertain it should be noted that it is a form known in ceramics wares prior to the Yongzheng period. Ceramic tripod vessels of very closely related shape can, in fact, be traced back to the Tang dynasty (*618-907*). For example see the dark brown glazed stoneware globular jar supported on three animal feet in the collection of the Denver Art Museum on loan from the Sze Hong Collection (*accession n° 100. 1989*) that is illustrated and discussed by *Robert D. Mowry* in ***Hare's Fur, Tortoiseshell and Partridge Feathers: Chinese Brown- and Black- Glazed Ceramics, 400-1400****, Harvard University Art Museum, 1996, page 87, n° 4.*

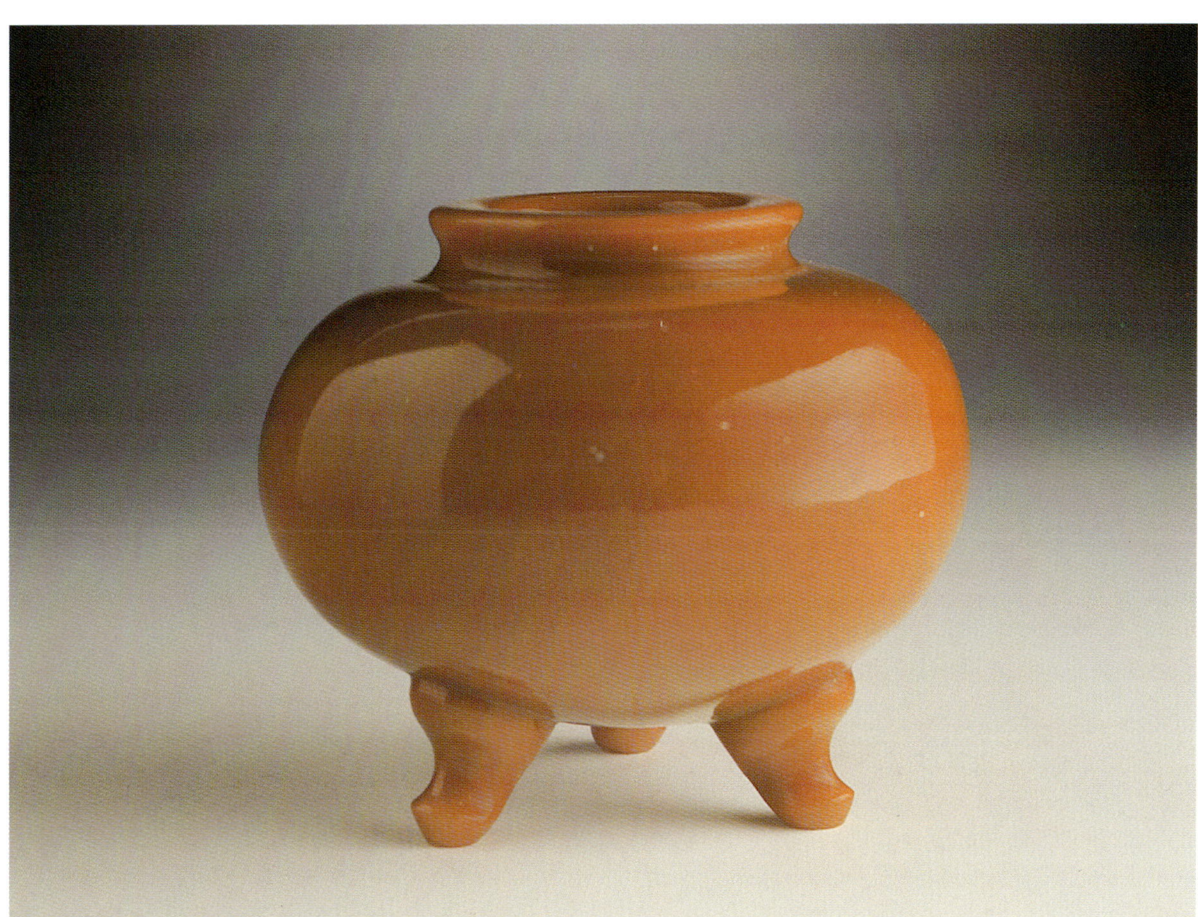

31

Vase

Opaque white glass spotted with red,
Late 19 th century
H: 18,8 cm

The **fairly thick walls** of this elegant amphora-shape vase curve gracefully upward from the small circular base, then turn sharply inward to form the flat shoulder from which rises a gently flared neck with a thickened rim. The lower portion of the neck is encircled by two raised bands. The opaque white glass is spotted with red in imitation of the porcelain glaze referred to as "peach bloom". The surface has a fairly mat appearance. The circular base is deeply concave and reveals the white grey color body.

At first, especially when viewed solely through a photograph, this vase appears like a perfect example of the influence of Chinese porcelain on Chinese glass production. Nearly identical examples, referred to as either **san xian ping** or **lai fu zun** in Chinese, are known in porcelain (see, for example, ***Kangxi, Yongzheng, Qianlong Qing Porcelain from the Palace Museum Collection***, *Beijing, Forbidden City Publishing House, The Woods Publishing Co., 1989, page 137, n° 120*). An other vase of this form is in the Collection of the Metropolitan Museum of Art (*accession number 50.145.286* see, ***Oriental Ceramics, The World's Great Collections***, *Kodansha International, Ltd., 1982, vol. 11, col. pl. 28*).

However, at closer inspection, the piece reveals several features suggesting the possibility of a non-Chinese origin. The glass has a mat, slightly rough surface rather than the smooth, highly tactile surface so characteristic of Chinese glass. The concave base is not finely finished and shows in the center a gray-white color body atypical of Chinese glass. The exterior 'peachbloom' color as well as the technique used to produce it are also unusual (compare the present vase with the glass 'peachbloom' peach-shape brush washer in the collection of *Mrs. Barney Dagen illustrated in Clarence Shangraw and Claudia Brown*, ***A Chorus of Colors: Chinese Glass from Three American Collections***, *exhibition catalogue, Asian Art Museum of San Francisco, 1995, page 102, cat n° 76*). Finally, and very significantly, the shape of the porcelain vase has not been quite accurately copied as only two, rather than the prescribed three, rings are depicted encircling the neck.

Then, one has to find where such a glass piece may have been produced. Unexpectedly, the answer seems to be in the United States in the late nineteenth century in reaction to the contemporary interest in Chinese "peachbloom" porcelain. This interest was primarily instigated by William Walter's purchase in 1886 of a 'peachbloom' porcelain vase of this form, previously in the collection of Mrs. Mary J. Morgan, for a then extraordinary price. The possibility of an American origin for this glass is further strengthened by the fact that a glass company in Wheeling, WV, produced glass versions of the Walter's vase (see, *Hiram W. Woodward, Jr.*, ***Asian Art in the Walters Art gallery: A Selection***, *Baltimore, 1991, page 62*).

Although this remarkable vase is full of surprises as to the nature of its material and its place of manufacture, its strong. aesthetic appeal is quite obvious.

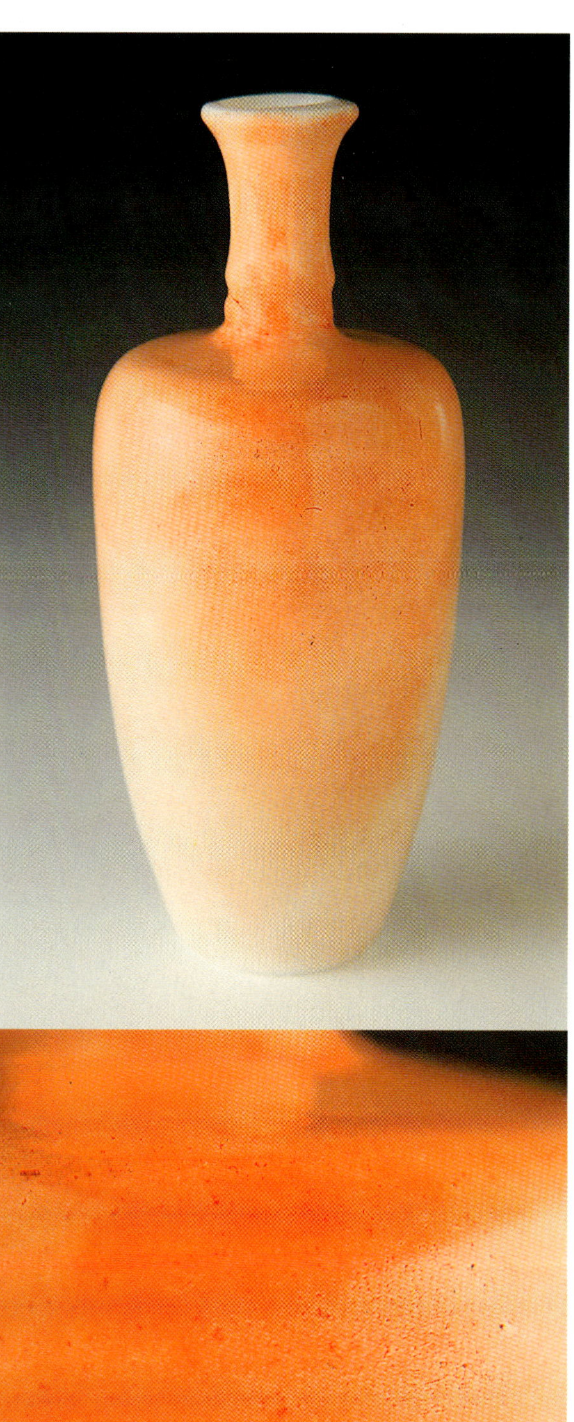

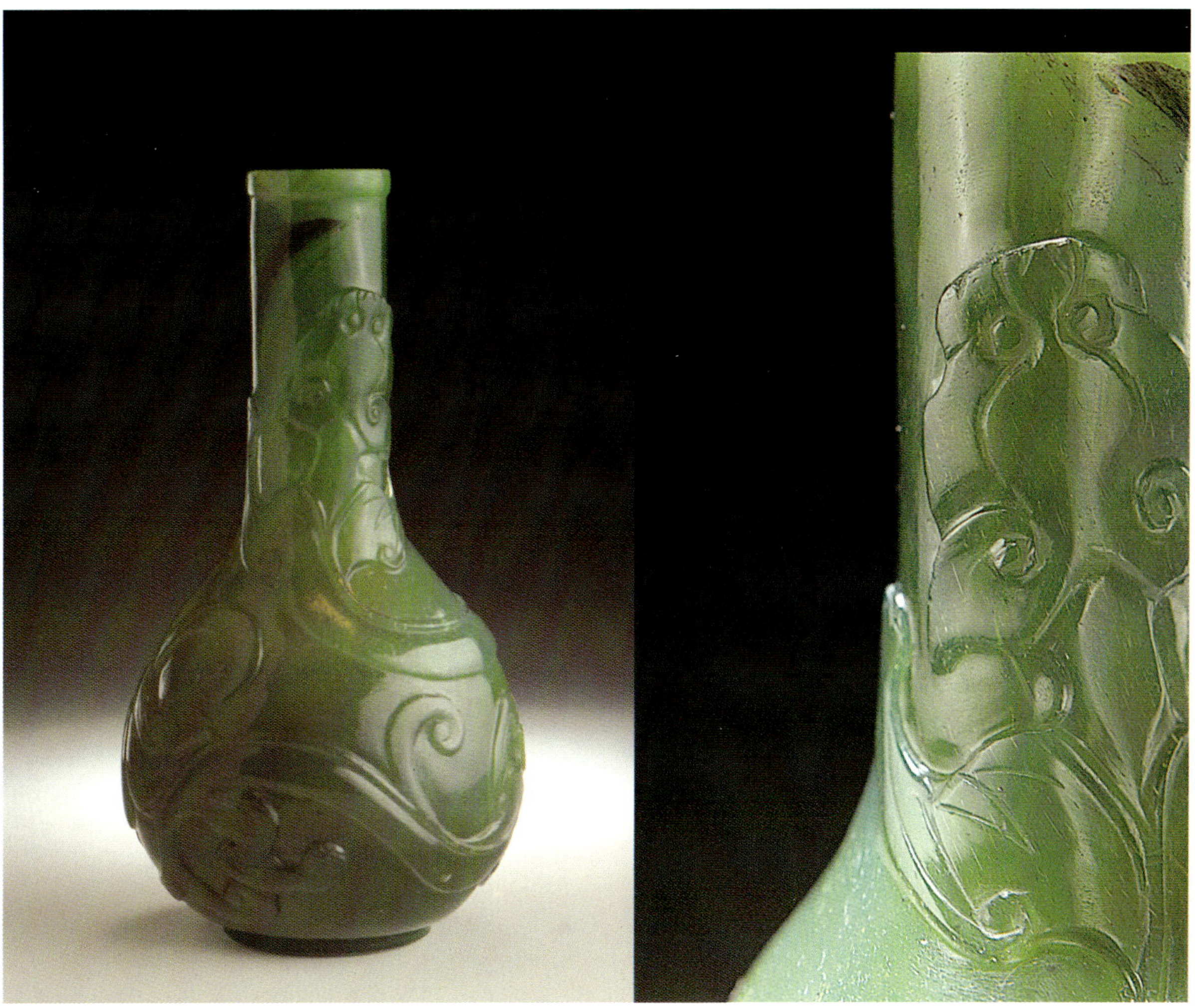

32

Vase

Translucent swirled green glass
Qing dynasty, 18 th century
H: 18,7 cm

This vase has an almost spherical body from which rises the tall, nearly cylindrical neck which has a wide rim. The finely carved design on the exterior depicts two **zhilong**. One entirely encircles the body of the vase and the second only partially encircles it as the **zhilong**'s head and front leg extend up one side of the neck. The carved forms are all of slightly rounded shapes and carefully finished. The vessel is supported on a relatively small, short foot ring with a beveled lower edge. The base is deeply recessed. The swirled glass has visible striations of opaque and transparent green color as well as a rather wide striation of nearly black color on the neck. The glass also has numerous small bubbles throughout.

The **zhilong** on this vase are portrayed with great dynamic energy and wonderfully fluid movement not usually associated with carved glass wares. The sinuous form of both **zhilong** compliments the rounded shape of the body of the vase and forces one's eyes to continuously move around the piece. A thin band or "spine" defines the outer edge of each **zhilong**'s body and emphasizes the sculptural presence of the subject. This relatively large vase is also surprisingly tactile for its size as the carved forms are all well rounded and smoothly finished. The two **zhilong**, in fact, seem to emerge from within the glass, a quality which is enhanced by carving the **zhilong** from the body of the vase rather than from a contrasting overlay color.

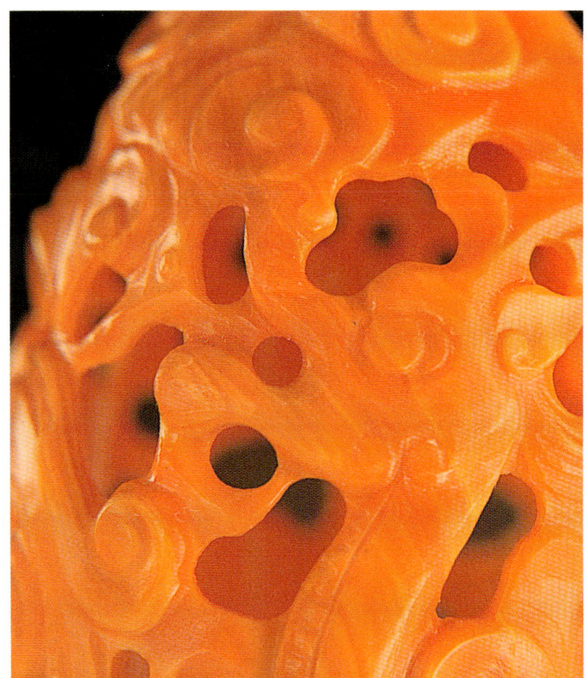

33

Openwork vase

Carved opaque orange glass
Qing dynasty, Qianlong period, 1736-95
H: 13,2 cm

This unusual small vase has a well formed ovoid body from which rises the cylindrical neck with a wide rim. The lip is deeply concave with a relatively small, circular mouth. The body is carved and pierced with a continuous design of two dragon-like animals among spiral shape motifs which represent either clouds or water. On one main side the dragon-like animal has its head turned back and on the opposite side its head faces forward. The foot ring is suggested by the gently tapered shape of the body and continues the spiral shape pattern, but the pattern is only carved and not pierced. The underside has a wide foot ring that surrounds a deeply recessed base. The glass consists of swirled tones of opaque orange color.

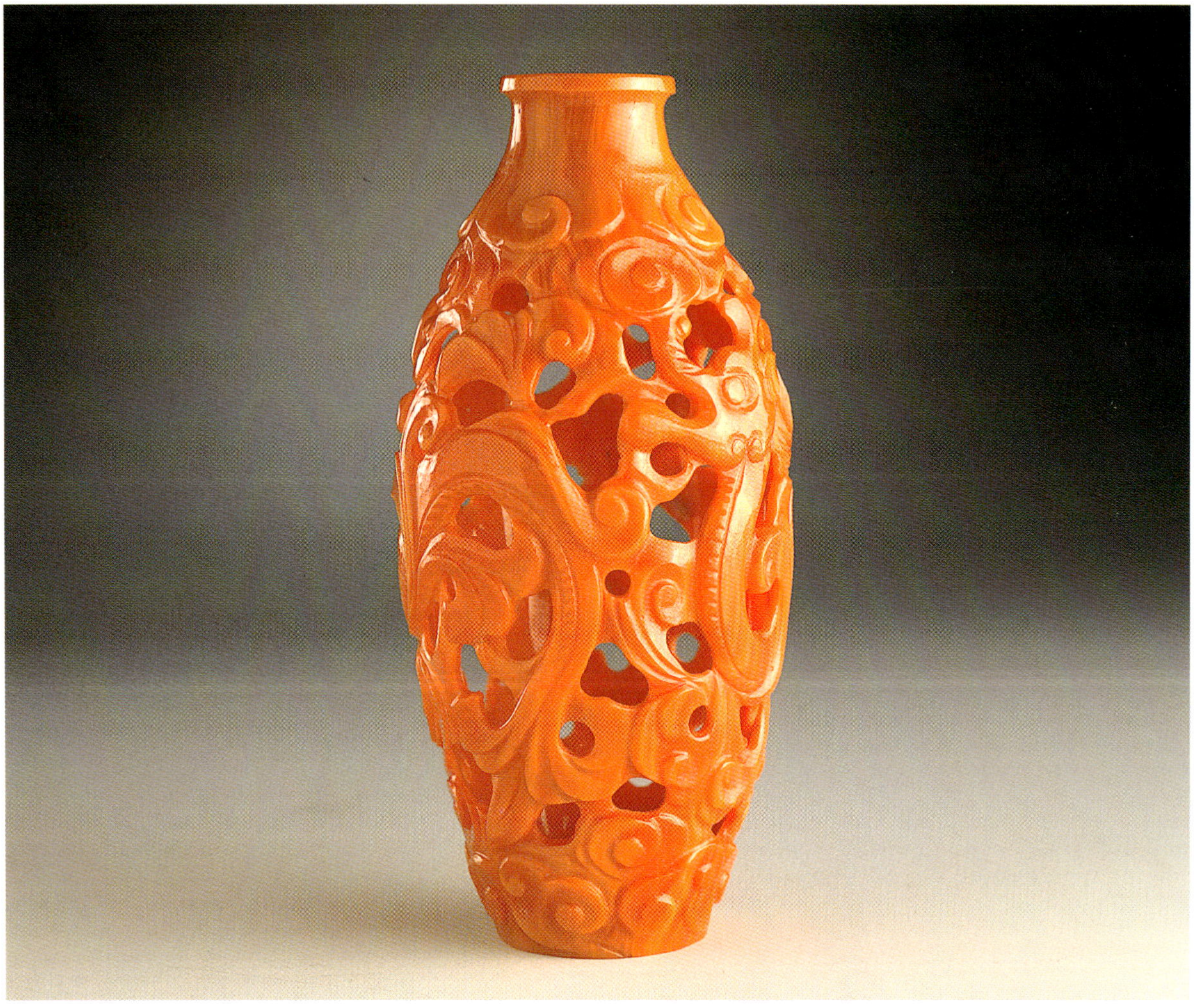

The virtuoso openwork carving displayed by this elegant vase exemplifies the wide experimentation and innovation during the eighteenth century with various decorative techniques in glass. Openwork carving was especially prevalent during the Qianlong period and its popularity is reflected in a number of media including porcelain (for a Qianlong mark and period porcelain vase that includes an openwork section of very similar subject and design see, ***Kangxi, Yongzheng, Qianlong Qing Porcelain from the Palace Collection***, Beijing, Forbidden City Publishing House. *The Woods Publishing Co, 1989, n° 116*) and painted enamels on metal (for a Qianlong period brazier with a painted enamel on metal openwork cover with a floral motif, see ***Tributes from Guangdong to the Qing Court***, *exhibition catalogue, Jointly presented by the Palace Museum, Beijing and the Art Gallery, The Chinese University of Hong Kong, 1987, page 82, n° 41*).

Glass openwork pieces are, however, relatively rare. For another openwork vase also carved from an opaque swirled orange glass, but of double gourd form see, Christie's, ***Fine Chinese Ceramics, Jades and Works of Art***, *New York, May 30, 1991, n° 97*. The carving technique employed on the related example is very similar to that of the present vase, and both might have come from the same workshop.

34

Vase

Bubble-suffused snowflake white glass with carved overlay of transparent red
Qing dynasty, 18 th century
H: 18,3 cm

This vase has a small bulbous body from which rises the tall, slightly tapered cylindrical neck with a wide rim carved from the overlay color. The body is formed from a colorless glass suffused with tiny bubbles and numerous small white 'snowflake' inclusions cased with transparent red and finely carved cameo style to represent a large peach tree springing decidedly from a rock work base. The body is supported on a relatively short foot ring carved from the overlay color. The base is slightly recessed.

Cased or overlay glass (**tao liao**) is mentioned as early as the Kangxi period (see Yang Boda, "A Brief Account of Qing Dynasty Glass," in *Claudia Brown and Donald Rabiner*, ***Chinese Glass of the Qing Dynasty, 1644-1911: The Robert H. Clague Collection***, *page 77*). The carved overlay represented by the present example, however, appears to be of the type described by Zhao Zhigian as being produced in the Qianlong period and called **pi** (skin) type (see, Richard John Lynn trans., "Researches Done During Spare Time into the Realm of Yong Lu God of the Nose, ***The Yonglu Xianjie*** of *Zhao Zhigian*", the ***Journal of the International Chinese Snuff Bottle Society***, *1991, volume XXIII, n° 3, page 17*).

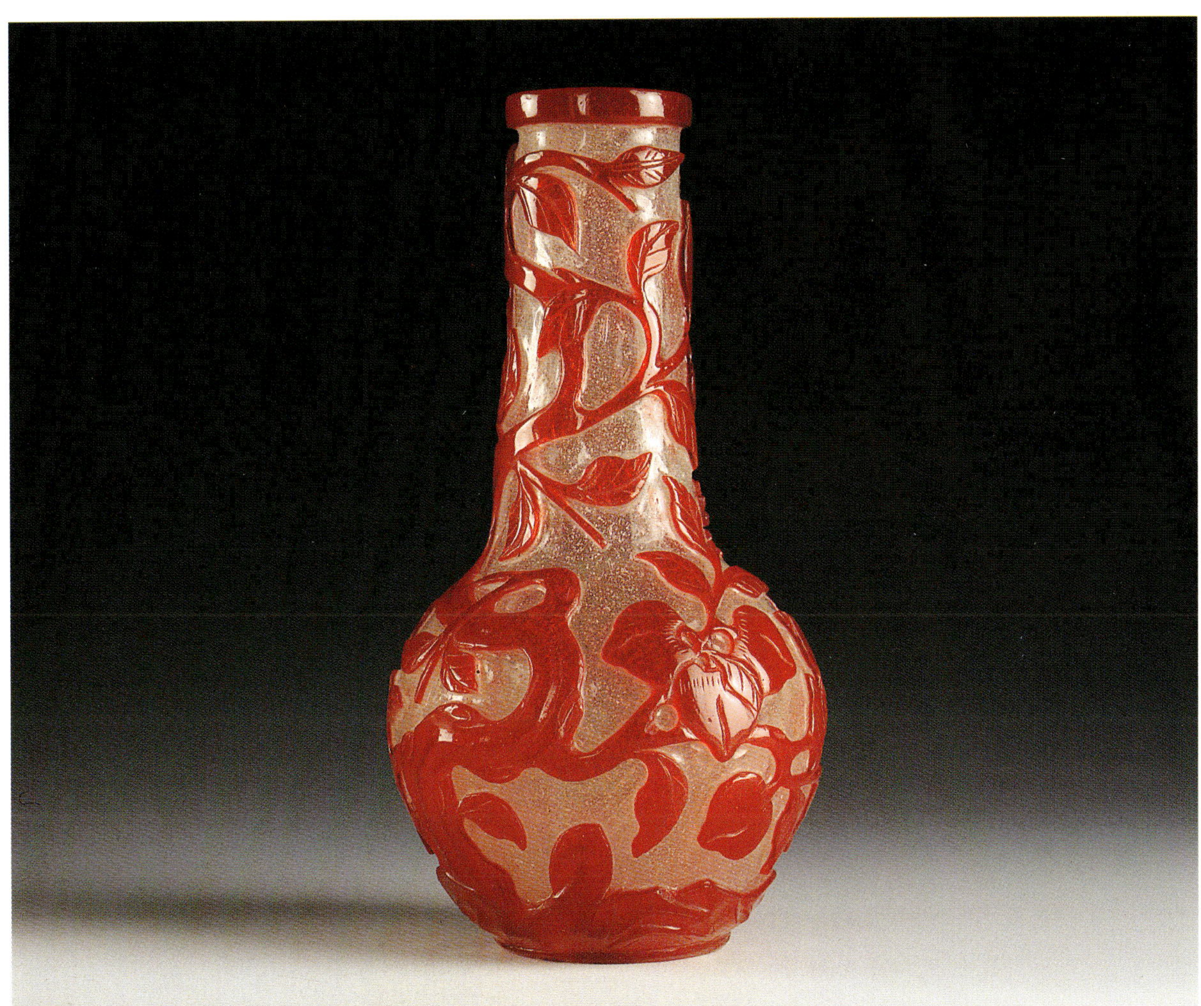

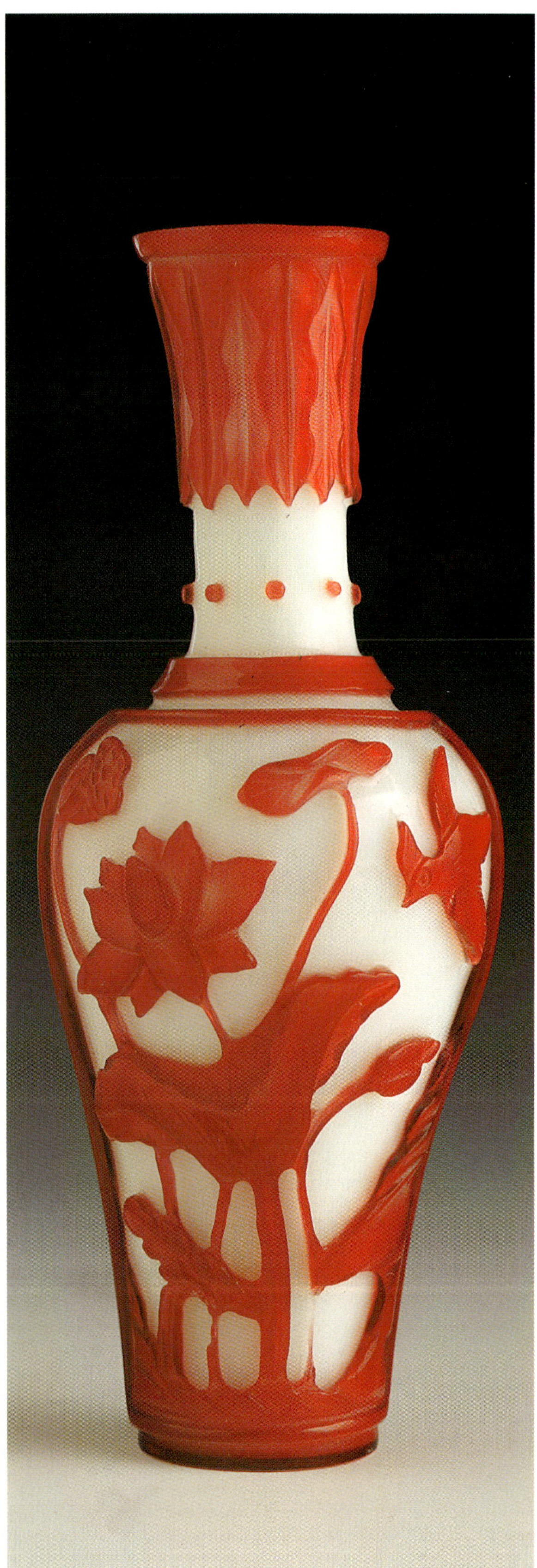

35

Vase

Opaque white glass with carved overlay of transparent red
Qing dynasty, late 18 th - 19 th century
H: 18,6 cm

This elegant vase has a **meiping**-shape body and a long, nearly cylindrical neck flaring slightly toward the top. The body is formed from opaque white glass cased with transparent red and carved cameo style to represent two large panels, one containing orchid blossoms and leaves as well as a butterfly whereas the opposite panel contains lotus blossoms and leaves as well as a bird. The overlay on the neck is delicately carved to represent overlapping pendent stylized leaves below the rim, a row of tiny bosses on the lower portion and a wide band at its base. The body is supported on a relatively short foot ring carved from the overlay. The base is deeply recessed.

36

Pair of vases

Opaque white glass with carved overlay of transparent red
Qing dynasty, 18 th century
H: 17,7 cm

Each of the vases in this pair has a fairly short cylindrical body that tapers toward the base and a nearly cylindrical neck with a wide rim carved from the overlay color. The body is formed from a fairly thick, opaque white glass and cased with a transparent red and carved cameo style to represent a blossoming prunus tree, bamboo, pierced rocks and several small birds. The vases depict this design in matched mirror image. The underside has a wide foot ring carved from the overlay that surrounds a deeply recessed base.

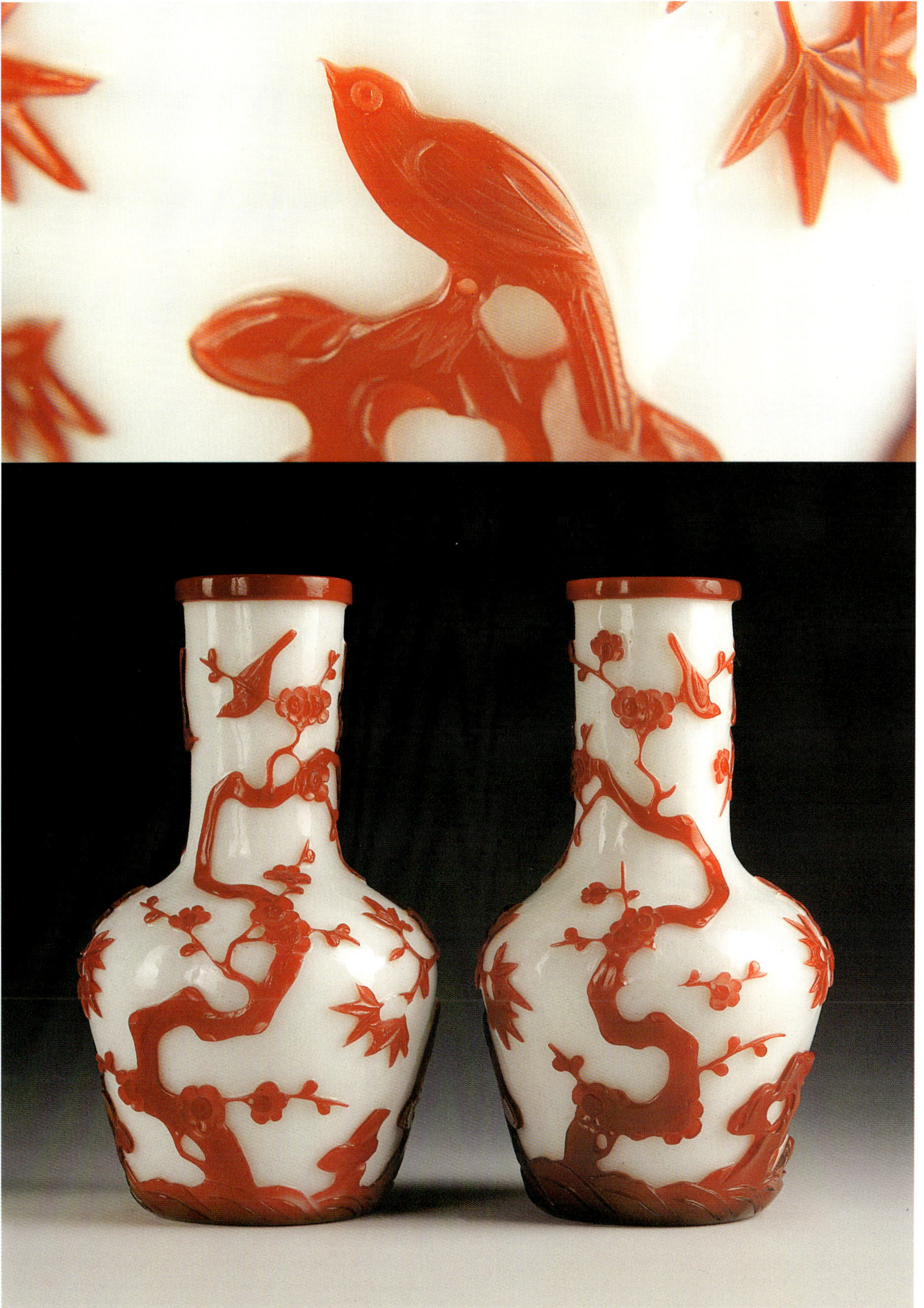

37

Vase of pear shape

Opaque white glass with carved overlay of opaque red
Qing dynasty, Qianlong mark and period, 1736-95
H: 18,2 cm

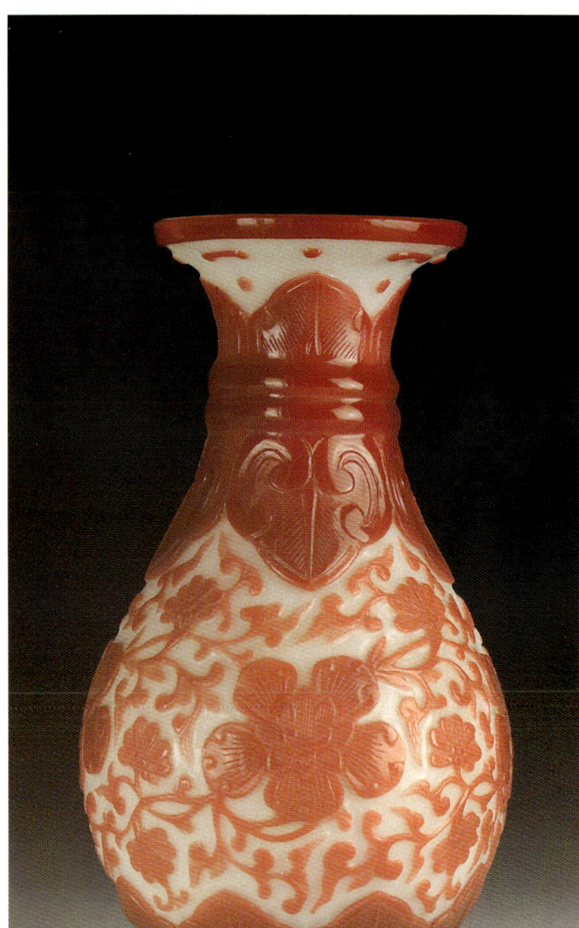

This pear-shape vase has an ovoid body from which rises the widely flared neck. The shape appears to have been formed in a mold as a thin seam is visible on the narrow edges. The body is formed from a fairly thick, opaque white glass cased with pink-red and exquisitely carved cameo style to represent an intricate pattern of peony blossoms and leaves. A band of upright leaves encloses the lower portion of the body. The neck is carved with large stylized leaves that are encircled by two bands at the mid-section of the neck. A small oval shape is carved through the overlay above as well as below the double band on the narrow edges and reveals the white body. The edge of the lip is enclosed by a rim carved from the overlay color and the underside of the flared lip is decorated with raised bosses and comma shape motifs. The body is supported on a high, slightly splayed foot ring of pink-red glass that has been fused-on separately to the body. The mark **Qianlong nian zhi** is incised in standard script along the periphery of the flat base.

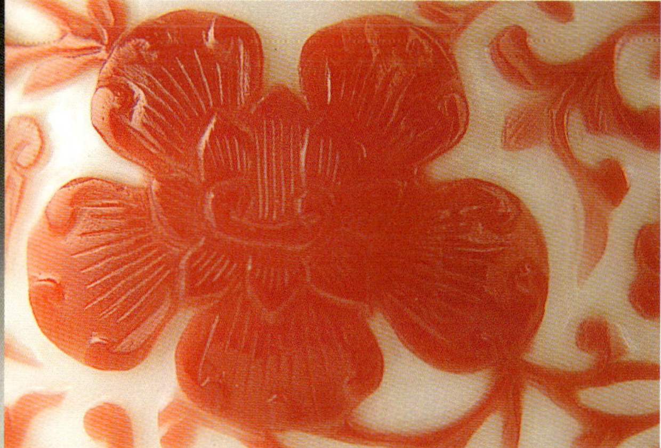

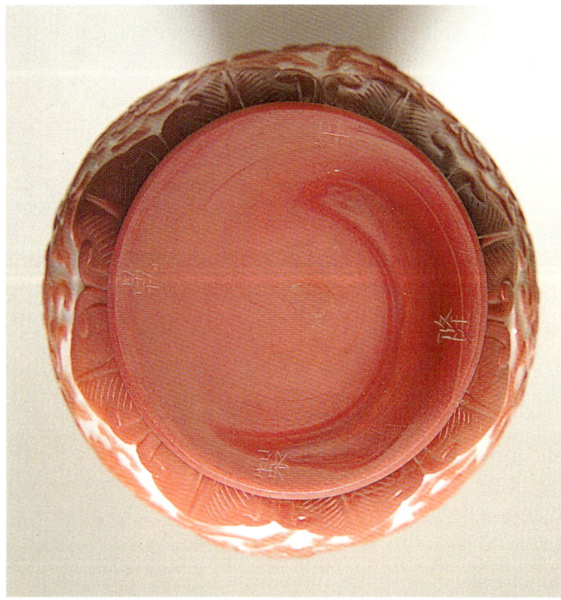

The shape, decoration and overlay of this elegant yet powerful glass vase appear to be directly inspired by underglaze copper red porcelains. For underglaze copper red decorated porcelain examples of closely related shape and decoration illustrating this similarity see, **Kangxi, Yongzheng, Qianlong Qing Porcelain from the Palace Museum Collection**, *Beijing, Forbidden City Publishing House, The Woods Publishing Co., 1989, no° 19*, for a Qing example and also see, **The Tsui Museum of Art**, *Hong Kong, 1991, n° 59, for a Ming period example.*

This vase belongs to a relatively small and fairly coherent group of Qianlong period cased glass wares that share several characteristics. These include: 1. extremely fine workmanship, 2. a distinct type of overlay which was produced in a variety of colors but has a consistent appearance, 3. low relief carving, 4. a solid "backed-on" foot ring and 5. perhaps the most distinct feature which is the manner in which the four character Qianlong mark is carved around the periphery of the flat base. For related examples that also belong to the group see, *Claudia Brown and Donald Rabiner,* ***Chinese Glass of the Qing Dynasty, 1644-1911: The Robert H. Clague Collection****, exhibition catalogue, Phoenix Art Museum, 1987, page 27, cat. n° 17* also illustrated on the cover. An other

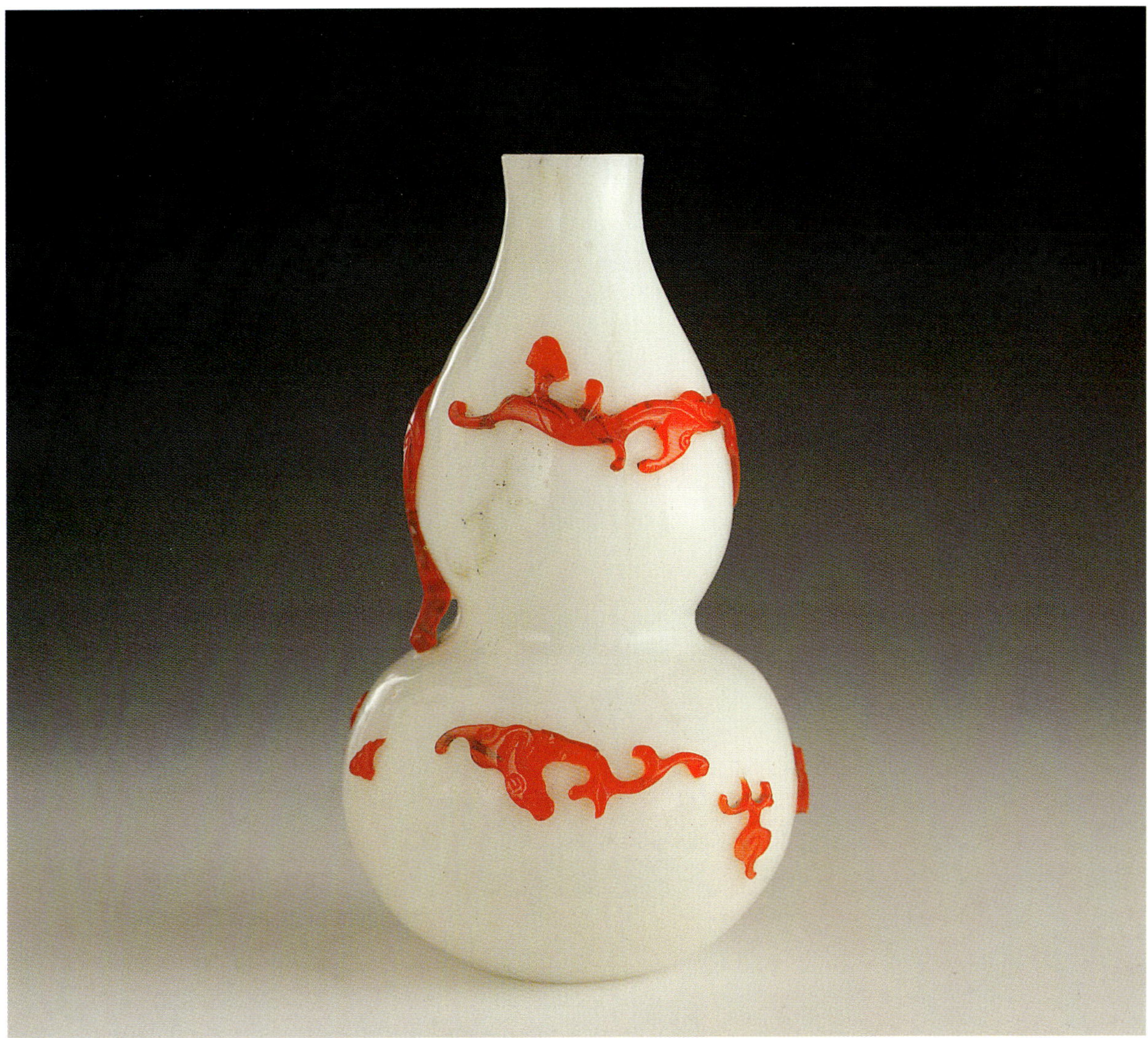

example is illustrated in Sotheby Parke Bernet, ***A Collection of Chinese Pekin Glass: The Property of Professor P. H. and Mrs. T. Plesch****, London, 1979, n° 81.*

It is, however important to note that the solid "backed-on" foot ring and the unusual composition of the mark while characteristic of this small cased glass group are not exclusive to it. One of the exceptions is a vase of "striped" glass in the Collection of the Palace Museum in Beijing which also includes these two distinct features but is not cased or carved as is typical of the group (see *Donald Rabiner, "Chinese Glass and the West" in Clarence Shangraw and Claudia Brown,* ***A Chorus of Colors: Chinese Glass from Three American Collections****, exhibition catalogue, Asian Art Museum of San Francisco, 1995, page 25, n° 6).*

38

Gourd-shaped vase

Striated opaque white glass with carved overlay of transparent red
Qing dynasty, 18 th century
H: 13,8 cm

The body of this small vase is carved as a double-gourd, with a compressed lower bulb and a more elongated, slightly ovoid shape, upper bulb. The cylindrical neck is gently flared. The body is formed from a thick, opaque glass that is primarily of white color but has several thin striations of green throughout. Overlays of transparent red are individually applied to the ground and carved as five **zhilong** and as small **ruyi** shape clouds. The circular base is flat.

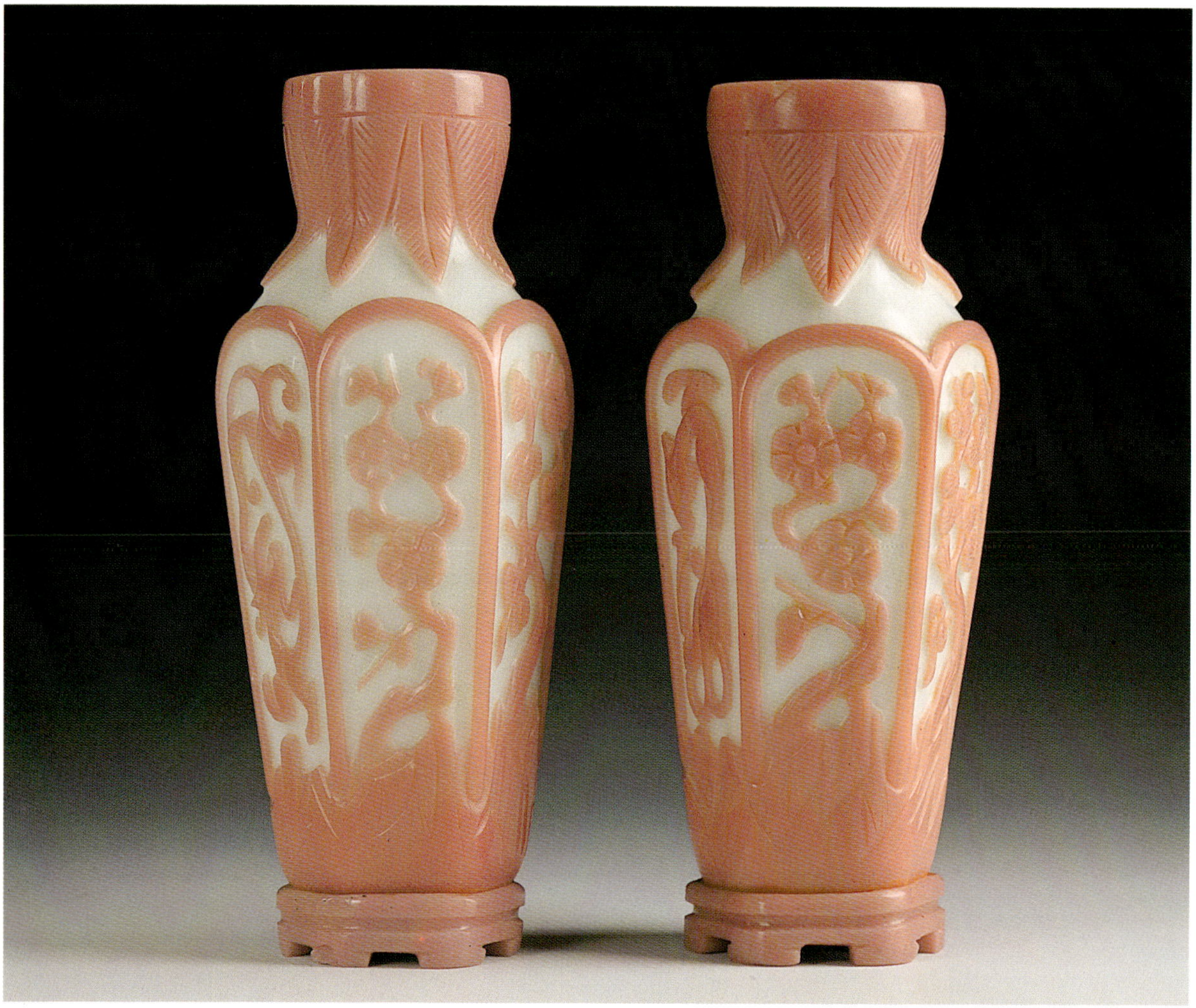

39

Pair of vases of hexagonal section

Opaque white glass with carved overlay of opaque pink
Qing dynasty, 19 th century
H: 19,9 cm

This **pair of vases** each has a six-sided body that gently tapers toward the base. The broad cylindrical neck flares slightly upward, then turns gently inward at the rim. The body is formed from an opaque white glass cased with opaque pink and carved cameo style. The six sides are carved as individual petal shape panels that are partially concealed by a continuous band of rock work. The six motifs contained in the panels are pine, bamboo, orchid, plum blossom, an ascending **zhilong** and a descending **zhilong**. The relatively high foot is of hexagonal shape, has a thin central band that is slightly recessed and is supported by six small rectangular feet.

For a blue overlay vase of related shape and design, but with a square foot, see *Claudia Brown and Donald Rabiner,* ***Chinese Glass of the Qing Dynasty, 1644-1911: The Robert H. Clague Collection****, exhibition catalogue, Phoenix Art Museum, 1987, page 35, cat. n° 31.*

The unusual treatment of the foot is similar to that on a pair of red and yellow covered jars also in the Clague Collection, *page 33, n° 28,* as well as a pair of red on yellow vases illustrated in Spink and Son, Ltd., ***Chinese Jewellery, Accessories and Glass,*** *London, 1991, page 71, n° 120.* The foot is most likely intended to represent

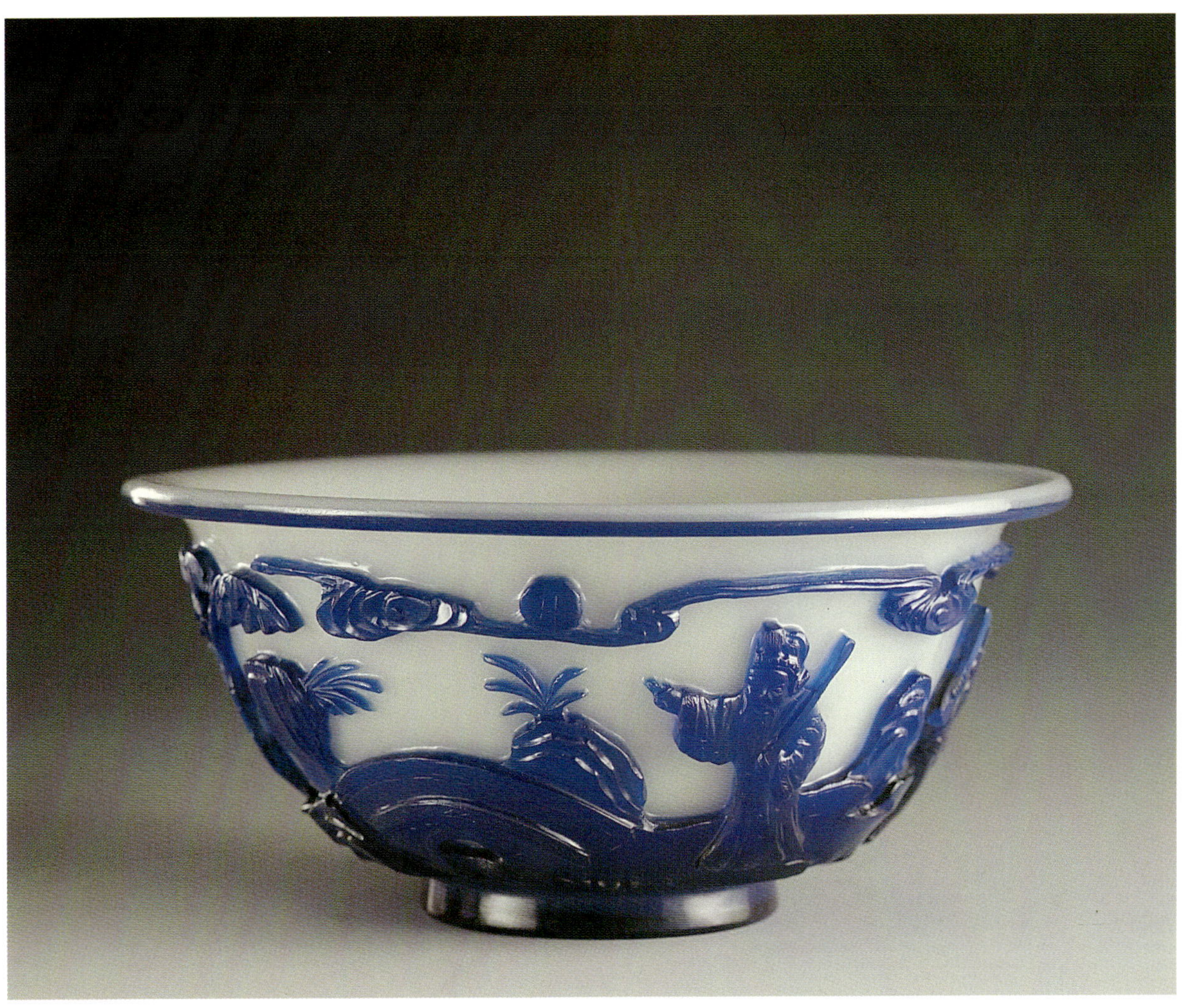

40

Bowl

Opaque white glass with carved overlay of transparent blue
Qing dynasty, 19 th century
Diam: 16,9 cm

a stand as its shape closely resembles the fitted hardwood stand which often accompanies glass pieces. For example, see the glass vase in the collection of Mrs. Barney Dagen illustrated on a hardwood stand of closely related shape in Claudia Brown and Donald Rabiner, **Clear as Crystal, Red as Flame: Later Chinese Glass**, *exhibition catalogue, New York: China House Gallery, China Institute of America, 1990, page 89, cat n° 55.*

This bowl has fairly thick, rounded walls that flare slightly outward and culminate in an everted rim the outer edge of which retains a portion of the overlay color. The body is formed from an opaque white glass cased with transparent blue and carved cameo style to represent a continuous landscape design that includes several figures. The bowl is supported on a high foot ring that is carved from the overlay color. The base is deeply recessed.

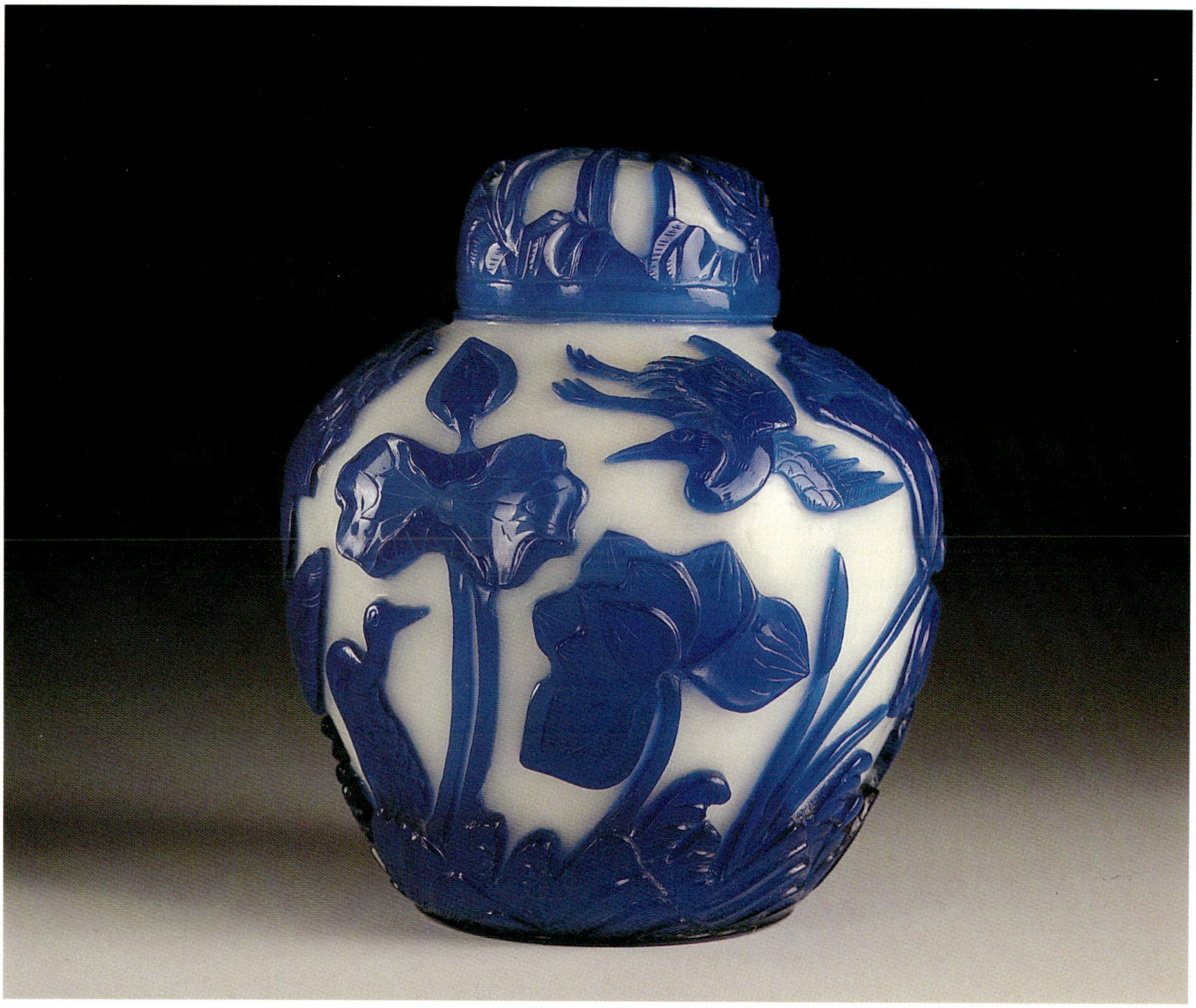

41

Covered jar

Opaque white glass with carved overlay of transparent blue
Qing dynasty, Qianlong mark but probably 19 th century
H: 14,1 cm

The rounded walls of this covered jar flare gently outward from the large circular base, then turn inward at the shoulder and ascend to a short cylindrical neck the base of which is encircled by a thin band carved from the overlay color. The body is formed from an opaque white glass cased with transparent blue and carved cameo style to represent lotus blossoms, leaves, several cranes and turbulent waves. The extremely short foot ring is carved from the overlay. The underside has a wide foot ring carved from the overlay that surrounds a deeply recessed base. The mark **Qianlong nian zhi** is incised in standard script within a double square on the base. The overlay on the dome shape cover is carved to represent continuous rock work and a **lingzhi** fungus.

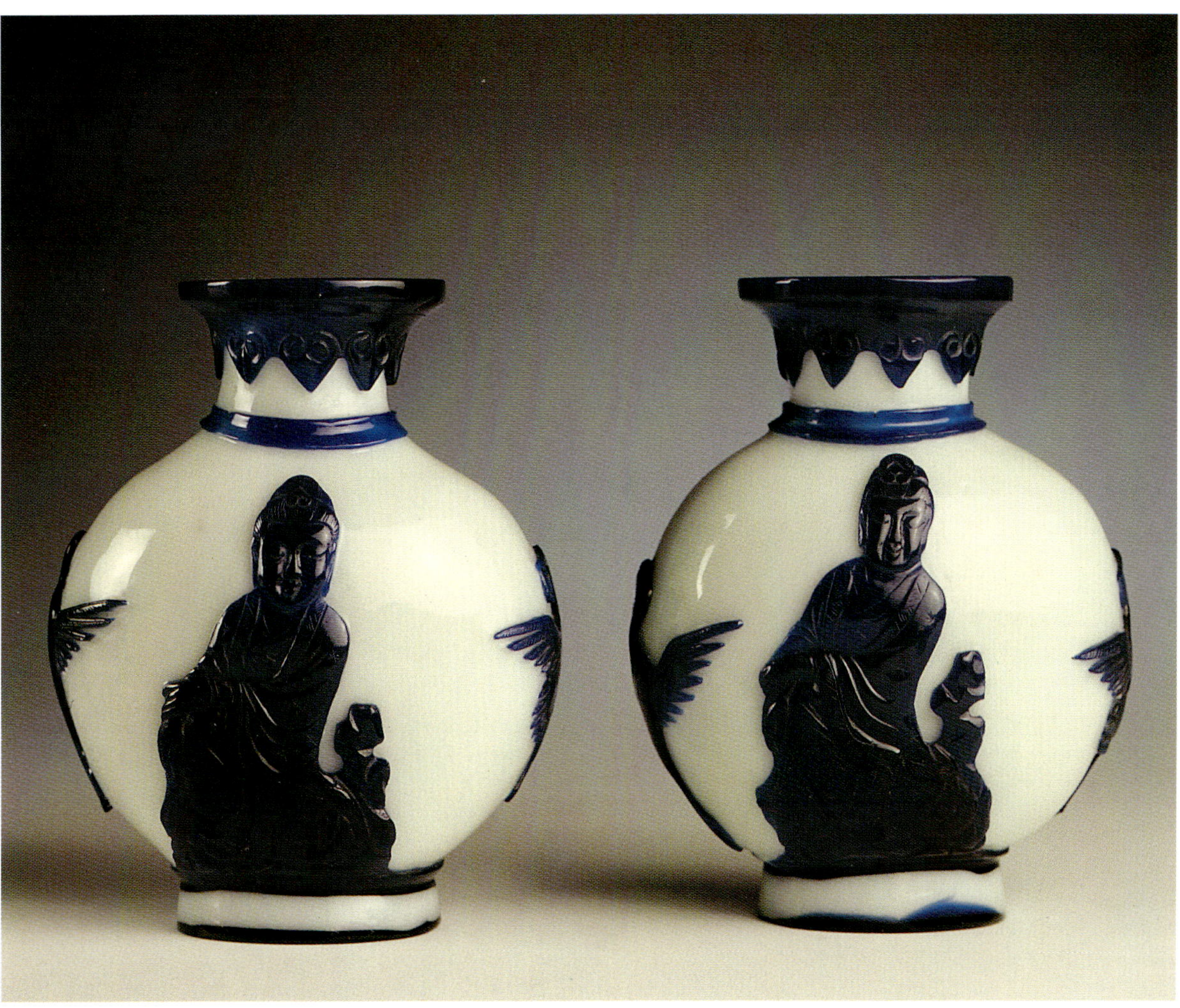

42

Pair of vases

Opaque white glass with carved overlay of transparent deep blue
Qing dynasty, Qianlong mark but 19 th century
H: 14,3 cm

Each of the vases of this pair has an almost circular shape body with flat main sides. The large cylindrical neck is gently flared and has a wide rim as well as a band of **ruyi** lappets carved from the overlay color. The body is formed from an opaque white glass cased with deep blue and carved cameo style with on one side, the figure of the bodhisattva Guanyin seated on a rock work and, on the opposite side, a Buddhist figure seated on a double lotus pedestal. The narrow sides each depict a large crane carved from the overlay. The body is supported on a high foot of oval shape carved from the white ground but retains traces of the overlay in the form of a narrow band on the upper and lower edge. The mark **Qianlong nian zhi** is incised in standard script within a double square on the deeply recessed base.

Buddhist figures are a relatively uncommon subject on cased glass vessels. For a Daoguang period snuff bottle of colorless glass cased with transparent green and carved cameo style to represent a Buddhist figure on both the main sides. See *Robert Kleiner, Yang Boda, Clarence F. Shangraw,* ***Chinese Snuff Bottles: A Miniature Art from the Collection of Mary and George Bloch****, exhibition catalogue, Hong Kong Museum of Art, 1994, page 181, n° 126.*

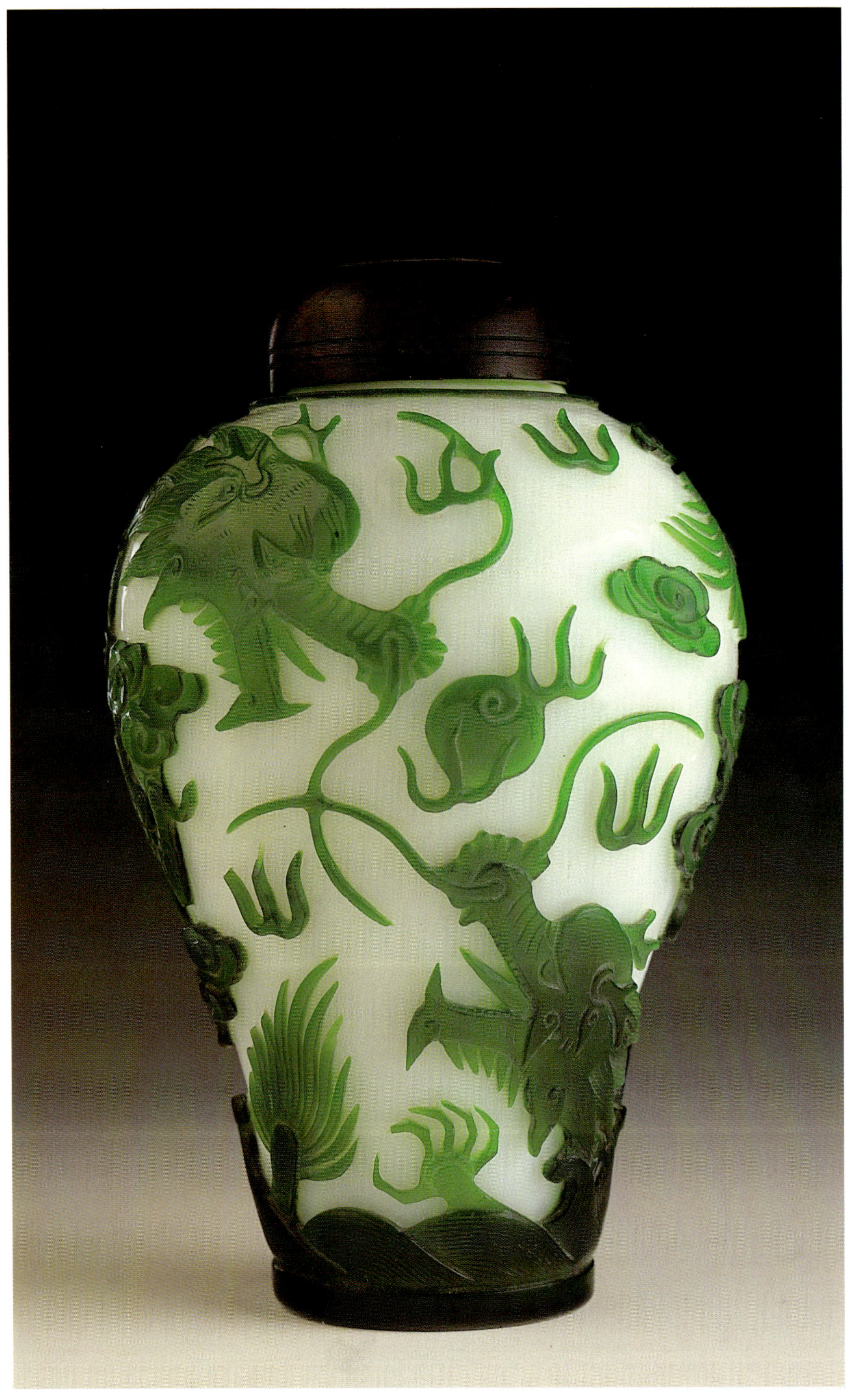

43

Bottle

Opaque white glass with carved overlay of transparent green
Possibly Qing dynasty or Republican period, late 19-20 th century
H: 18,3 cm

T**his covered bottle** has an elongated ovoid body with large bulging shoulders from which rises the short cylindrical neck. The body is formed from a thin, opaque white glass cased with transparent green and carved cameo style to represent two dragons confronting a flaming pearl and includes vigorous waves. Also carved from the overlay color at the base of the neck are two thin concentric bands to receive a lid. The present dome shape wood lid is most likely a replacement for a glass one. The body is supported on a relatively high foot ring that surrounds a slightly recessed base.

44

Covered jar

Opaque swirled yellow glass with carved overlay of transparent red
Qing dynasty, 18 th century
H: 18,8 cm

T**his large covered jar** has an almost spherical body from which rises the relatively short cylindrical neck. The body is formed from a swirled yellow glass cased with red and finely carved cameo style to represent a scrolling vine that bears numerous sinuous leaves and three large blossoms, possibly lotus. The central floral subject is enclosed on the upper edge by pendent **ruyi** lappets and, on the lower edge, by individual lotus panels. The body is supported on a relatively short foot ring carved from the yellow ground. The base is deeply recessed. The overlay on the dome shape cover is carved to represent a small central flower encircled by **ruyi** petals on the top, a thin band in the midsection and lotus panels around the lower edge.

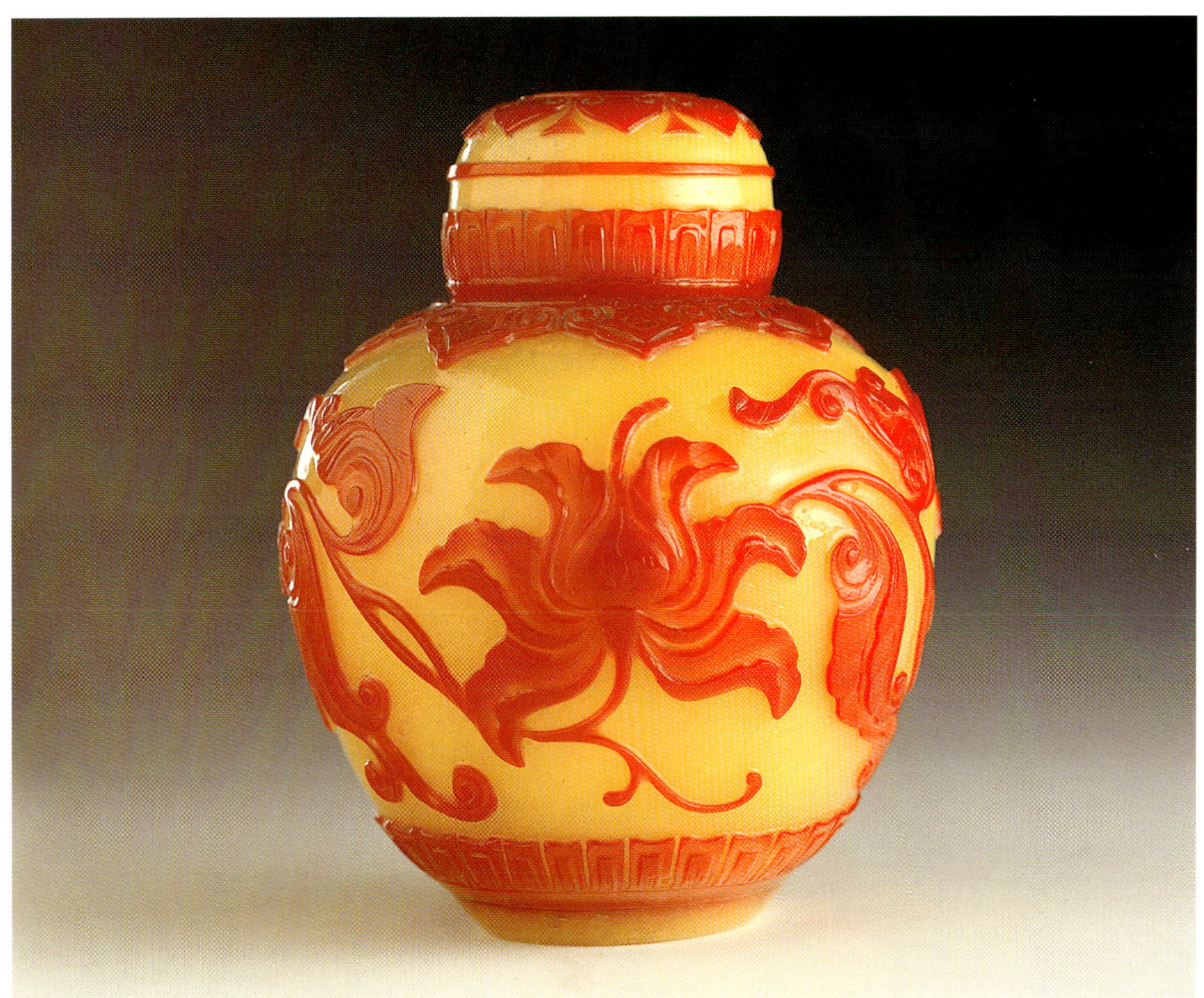

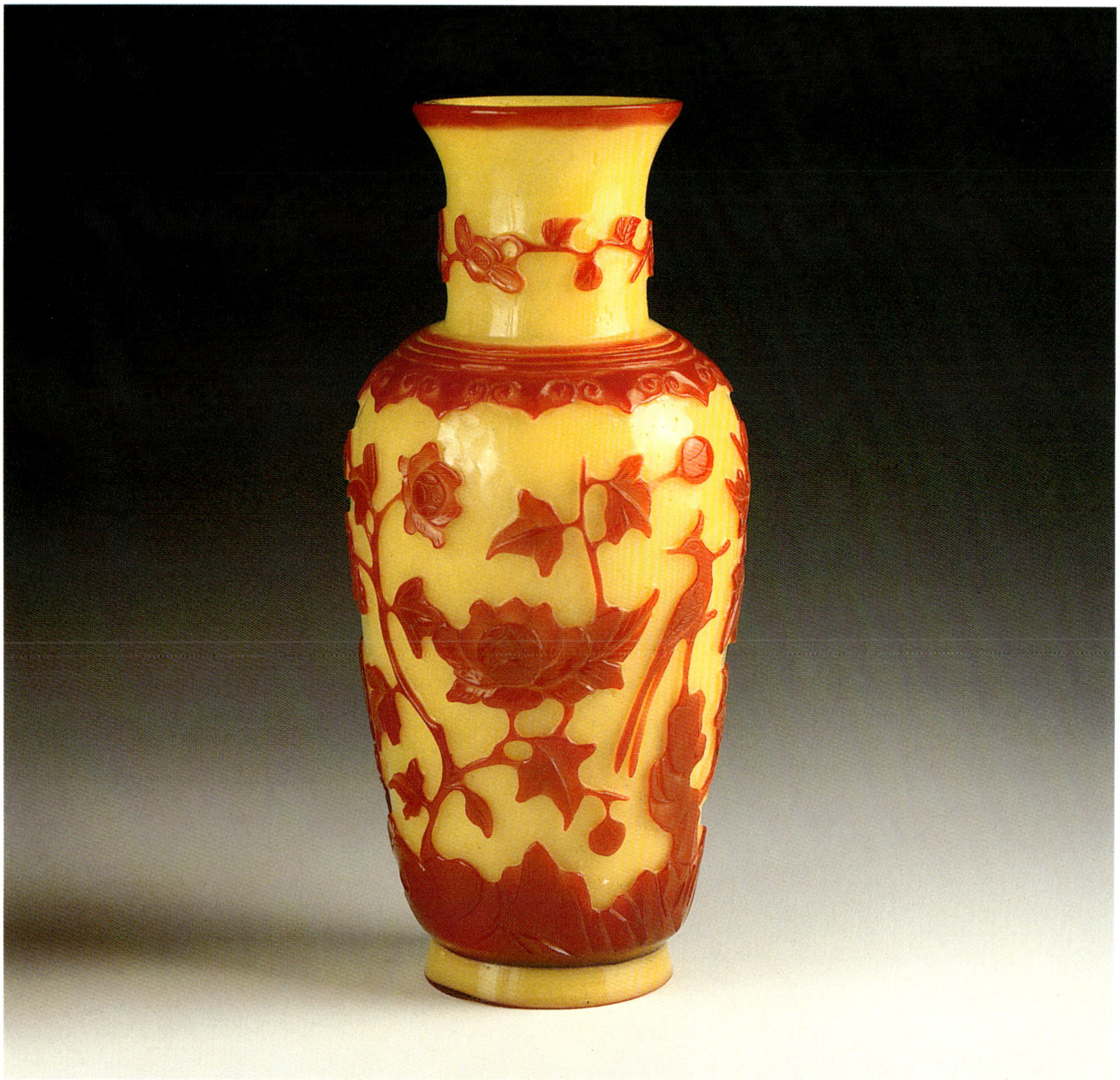

45

Vase

Opaque yellow glass with carved overlay of transparent red
Qing dynasty, 18 th - early 19th century
H: 19 cm
Provenance: Mr. and Mrs. William Arbeiter
Published: Berniece and Henry Blount,
***French Cameo Glass,** 1968, p.1246*
Wallace-Homestead Co, Des Moines, Iowa 1968, pl. 246

This vase has a cylindrical body that gently tapers toward the base and a broad cylindrical neck which flares slightly toward the top. The body is formed from an opaque yellow glass cased with transparent red and carved cameo style to represent a pair of phoenix among large peony flowers which spring from rock work. This scene is enclosed on the upper edge by **ruyi** lappets. The overlay on the neck is carved as a fairly wide rim around the mouth, a delicate flowering branch that encircles the midsection and as three concentric bands at the base. The body is supported on a relatively high, slightly splayed foot ring which is carved primarily from the yellow ground, but a thin band of the overlay color is visible at its lower edge. The underside has a wide foot carved from the overlay that surrounds a deeply recessed base.

A red over yellow glass vase carved cameo style with similar motifs is illustrated in Sotheby's, **Fine Chinese Ceramics, Furniture and Works of Art**, *New York, May 31 and June 1,1994, n° 181*. The related example includes the incised mark **Qianlong nian zhi** within a square on the base.

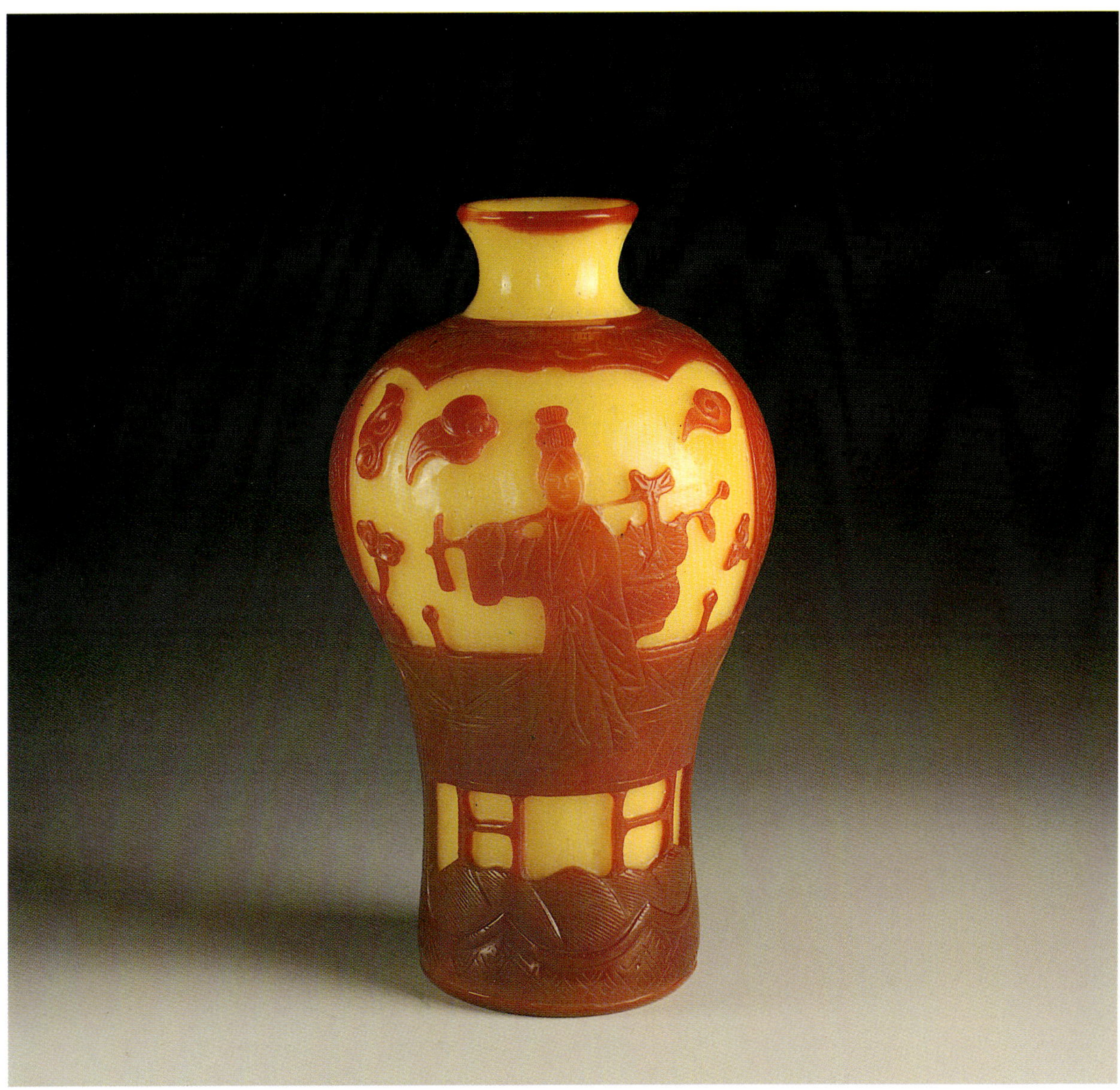

46

Vase of *meiping* shape

Opaque yellow glass with carved overlay of transparent red
Qing dynasty, 19 th century
Diam: 14,2 cm

The walls of this *meiping*-shape vase turn gently inward at the shoulder and ascend to a gracefully flared neck that has a thin, slightly uneven rim carved from the overlay color. The body is formed from a fairly thick, opaque yellow glass cased with transparent red. The body retains most of the overlay, except on the main sides which are both carved in cameo style with a pictorial panel and each contains a different scene representing a female immortal. The surrounding overlay is finely incised with a squared spiral pattern. The base is deeply recessed and enclosed by a wide foot ring carved from the overlay color.

47

Small dish

Carved of opaque blue-green glass with a carved overlay of opaque bright blue which primarily forms the foot ring
Qing dynasty, Qianlong period, 1736-1795
H: 10,3 cm

Elegant and beautifully shaped this small dish has a compressed circular shape lower body from which rises a larger, gently flared bowl shape section which opens to form a wide mouth. The smaller section is exquisitely carved with lotus panels. The interior of the dish corresponds to its exterior appearance. The glass is of opaque, swirled green color partially cased with opaque blue. The body is supported on a small, relatively high foot ring that is primarily carved from the overlay color. The base is deeply recessed.

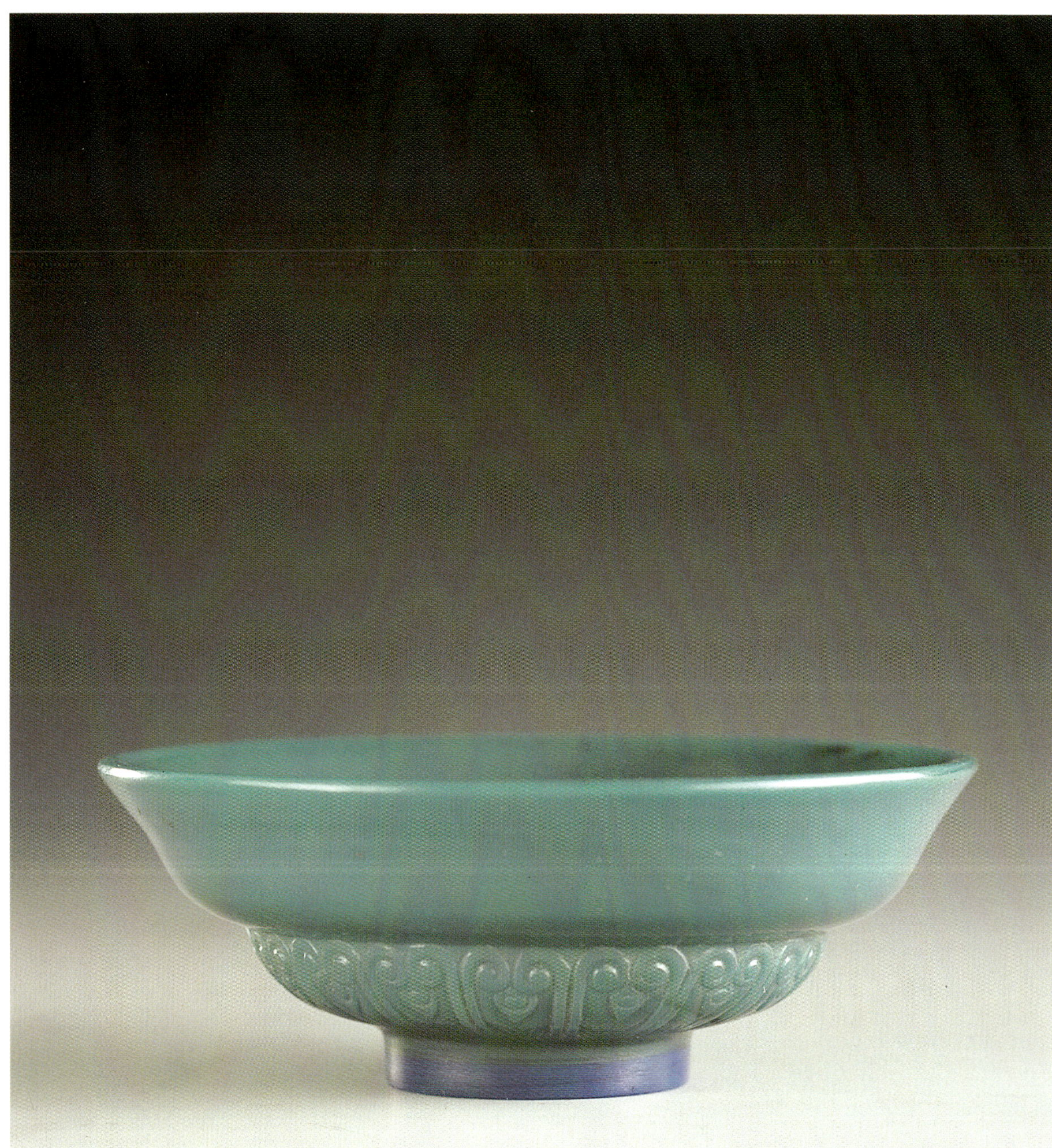

48

Vase

Snowflake white glass with carved overlays of transparent green and red as well as opaque yellow, pink, blue and brown
Qing dynasty, late 18 th - 19 th century
H: 14,9 cm

This vase has a bulbous body from which rises the tall, nearly cylindrical neck with a wide rim carved from the green overlay color. The body is formed from a colorless glass that is suffused with small white "snowflake" inclusions and cased with an overlay primarily consisting of transparent green color, but also includes smaller areas of red, yellow, pink, blue and brown. The various colors of the overlay have been carved cameo style in a continuous design that features three trees springing from rock work. The trees bear several large fruits, including peach, pomegranate and finger citron which are all carved from one of the bright colors of the overlay. The body is supported on an extremely short foot ring that is carved from the green overlay color. The base is deeply recessed.

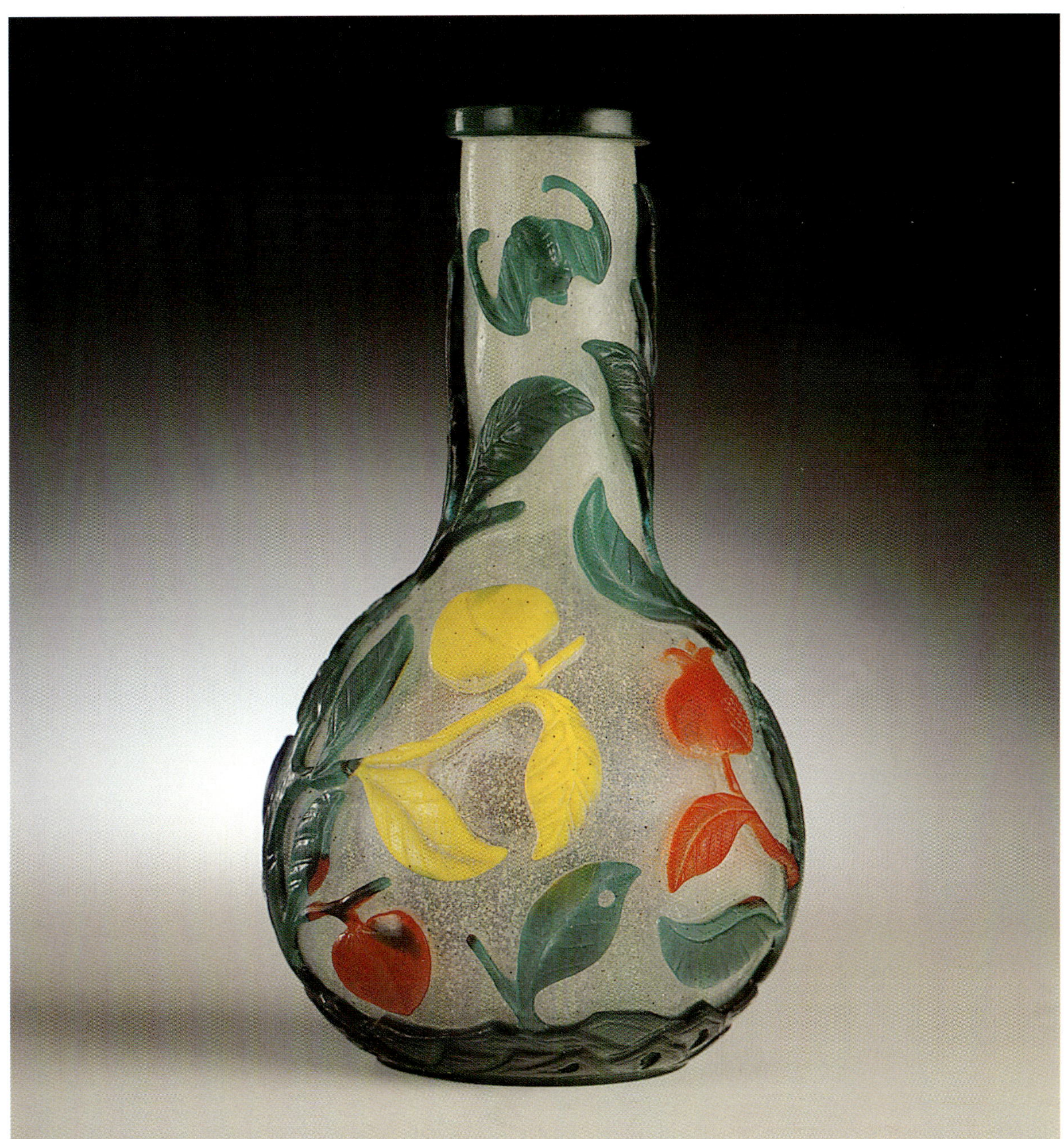

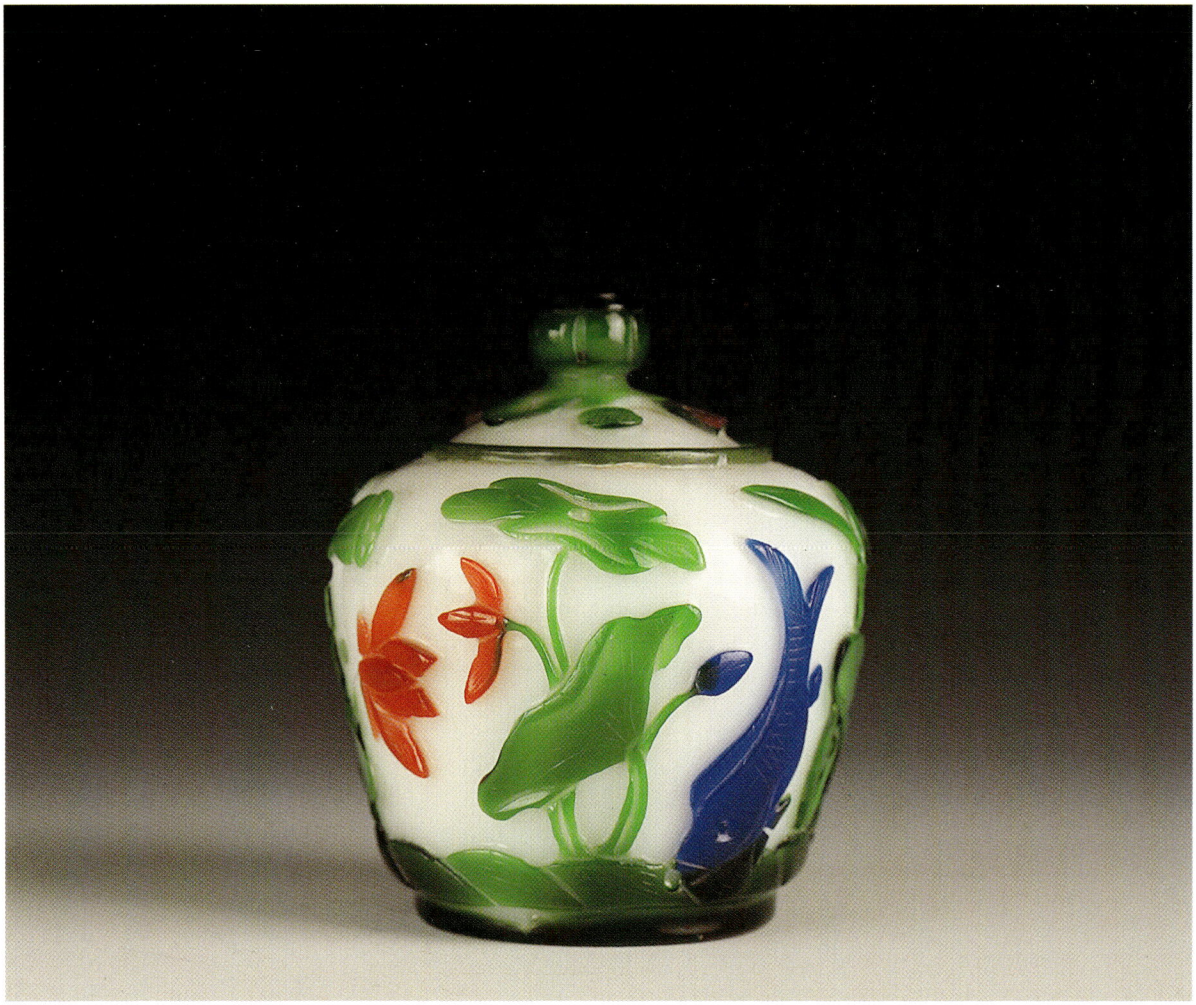

49

Small covered jar

Opaque white glass with carved overlays of transparent green, red and blue as well as opaque yellow and pink
Qing dynasty, 18 th - 19th century
H: 8,5 cm

The fairly thin, rounded walls of this small covered jar taper toward the base. The circular mouth is relatively large and is surrounded by a rim carved from the green overlay color. The body is formed from an opaque white glass cased with an overlay primarily consisting of transparent green color, but also includes red and blue as well as opaque yellow and pink. The various colors of the overlay are carved cameo style in a continuous design that features lotus blossoms, leaves, small waves and includes a large fish carved entirely from the blue overlay color. The body is supported on a short foot ring carved from the green overlay color. The base is slightly recessed. The conical shape cover is cased with red and green overlay colors and carved cameo style to represent lotus motifs. This color is surmounted by a small finial which is carved from the green overlay color to resemble a lotus pod.

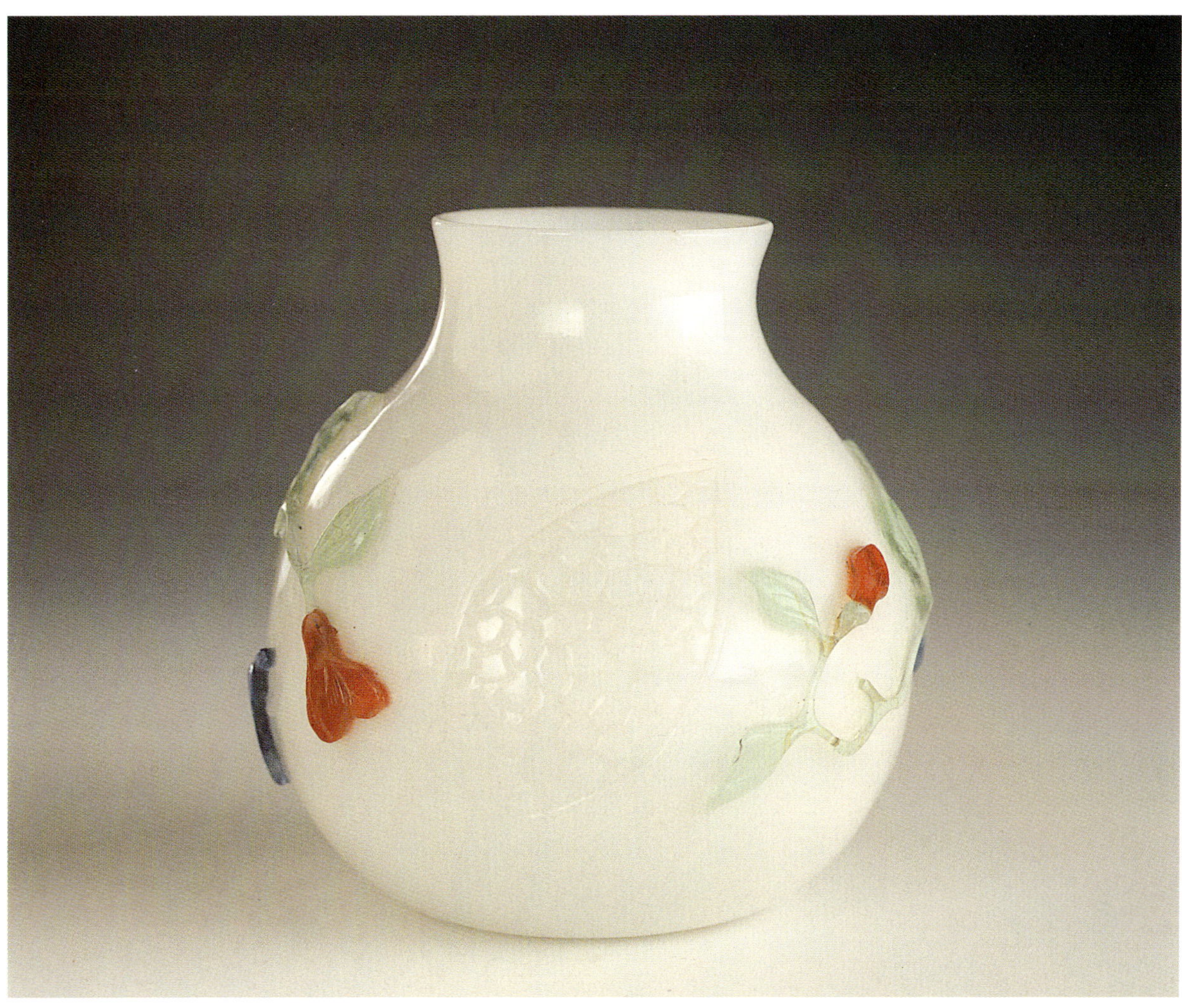

50

Jar in the shape of a pomegranate

Translucent white glass with carved overlays of transparent green, blue and red
Qing dynasty, 18 th century
Diam: 8,8 cm

The thin walls of this delicate jar curve outward, then turn gently inward and ascend to a gracefully flared neck. The well formed shape represents a pomegranate. The body is formed from a translucent white glass with some thin striations of colorless glass. The surface is smooth and lustrous. One side of the body is finely carved in shallow relief so as to suggest that one piece of the skin of the pomegranate has been peeled away, revealing a cluster of seeds. Overlays of transparent green, red and blue color have been individually and carefully applied and carved to represent two vines bearing flowers as well as a tiny pomegranate. Also included on the lower portion of the body is a three-legged toad carved from a blue overlay. The center of the circular base has a small concave recess that continues the suggestion of the shape of the fruit.

51

Vase with cut neck

Opaque white glass with carved overlays of transparent deep blue and red
Qing dynasty, 18 th century
H: 8,7 cm

This footed vessel has has a slightly compressed bulbous body and a small circular mouth which surrounds an even smaller recessed opening. The body is formed from a fairly thick, opaque white glass that is striated with pale pink swirls. Overlays of transparent red on one side and transparent blue on the opposite side have been individually applied and each carved to represent a **zhilong** and tiny clouds. The simulated ring handles with **taotie** masks are carved from a similar type of opaque white glass as the body of the vessel and applied to the surface of the narrow edges. The body is supported on a high, slightly splayed foot ring that surrounds a deeply recessed base.

The slightly compressed bulbous body of this footed vessel closely resembles the shape of a brush washer in the collection of Mrs. Barney Dagen (see, *Clarence Shangraw and Claudia Rabiner*, ***A Chorus of Colors: Chinese Glass from Three American Collections***, *exhibition catalogue, Asian Art Museum of San Francisco, 1995, page 105, cat. n° 79*). While the present vessel can be used as a brush washer certain features suggest that it was not intended originally to serve this function. The tall height and small size of the foot ring are atypical as most brush washers have either a relatively low and quite large foot ring or a flat base to give the form extra stability. The very high relief carving as represented by the mask and ring handles on the narrow edge is also unusual. The most revealing feature, however, is the unpolished circular opening with its slightly recessed lower rim which suggests that this vessel originally had a cylindrical neck. For an example of what this vessel may have looked like with its neck intact see, *Claudia Brown and Donald Rabiner*, ***Chinese Glass of the Qing Dynasty: 1644-1911: The Robert H. Clague Collection***, *exhibition catalogue, Phoenix Art Museum, 1987, page 29, cat n° 20*. The Clague Collection also includes a small water jar that appears to have originally been a vase (see *page 26, cat n° 16 as cited above*).

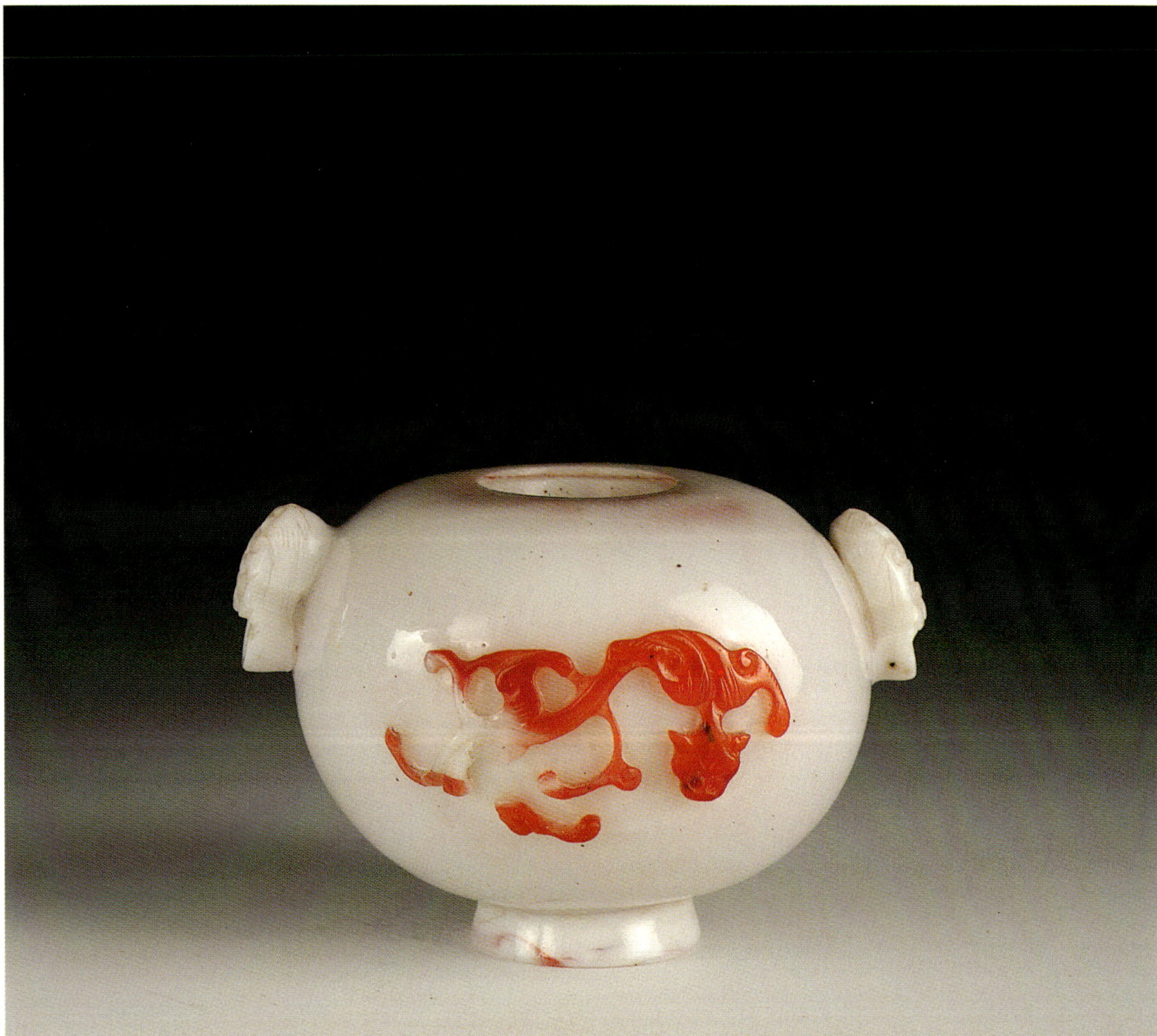

52

Vase of elongated *meiping*-shape

Transparent deep blue glass with carved overlays of opaque white
Qing dynasty, 18 th century
H: 15,2 cm

The walls of this elegant, elongated *meiping*-shape vase turn gently inward at the shoulder and ascend to a short cylindrical neck. The body is formed from a fairly thick, transparent, deep blue glass. The surface is smooth and well finished. Overlays, of opaque white color glass, have been applied to the ground and exquisitely carved to represent a spray of orchids as well as a twinning branch of blossoming prunus on one main side and a spray of chrysanthemum as well as a sinuous stem bearing several peonies on the opposite side. The body is supported on a delicate foot ring slightly smaller than the lower edge of the body accentuating the elegance of the vase. The base is deeply recessed.

This elegant vase reverses the more common color combination of a blue overlay on a white ground with spectacular results. The nineteenth century artist and. connoisseur, Zhao Zhigian records this color combination in his original draft of the **Yonglu Xianjie** completed between 1864 and 1868, stating that "White overlays might have a blue or green ground, or perhaps a black ground, but there are none with a red ground" (see Richard John Lynn, trans., 'Researches Done During Spare Time into the Realm of Yong Lu God of the Nose. The **Yonglu Xianjie** of *Zhao Zhigian'*, in the ***Journal of the International Chinese Snuff Bottle Society****, 1991, volume XXIII, n° 3, page 17*).

Technically and stylistically this small vase is closely related to a snuff bottle illustrated in ***Zhongguo biyanhu zhenshang***, edited by *Geng Baochang and Zhao Binghua, Hong Kong, Joint Publishing and Taikong Culture Enterprise, 1992 page 88, n° 85*. This related snuff bottle also has a transparent dark blue ground cased with an opaque white overlay carved cameo style to represent a design that includes various types of flowers. The carving technique employed on the snuff bottle is similar to that of the present vase, even in such details as the manner in which the stems, leaves and flowers are depicted, and suggests that both may have come from the same workshop or from contemporaneous workshops in the same area.

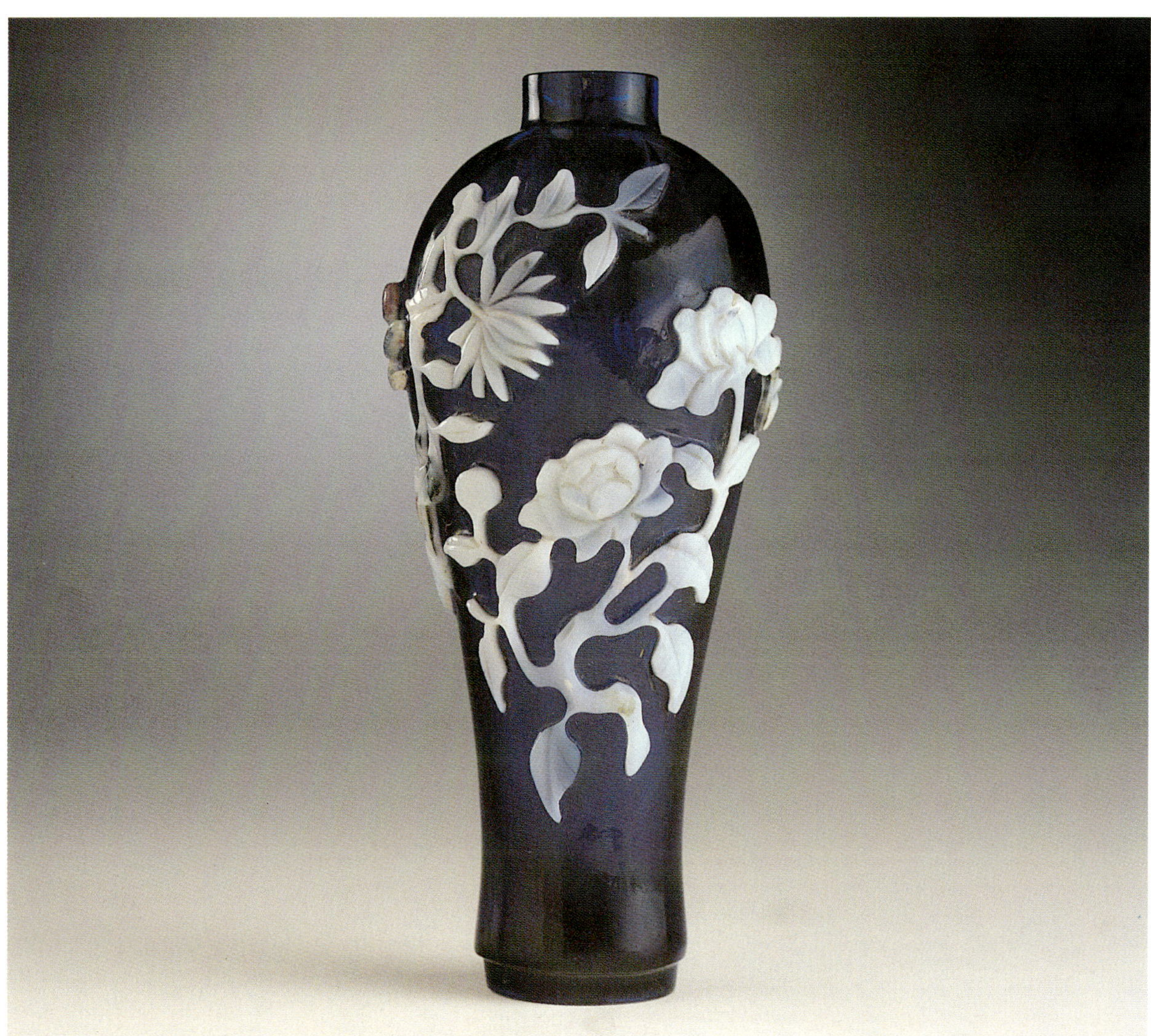

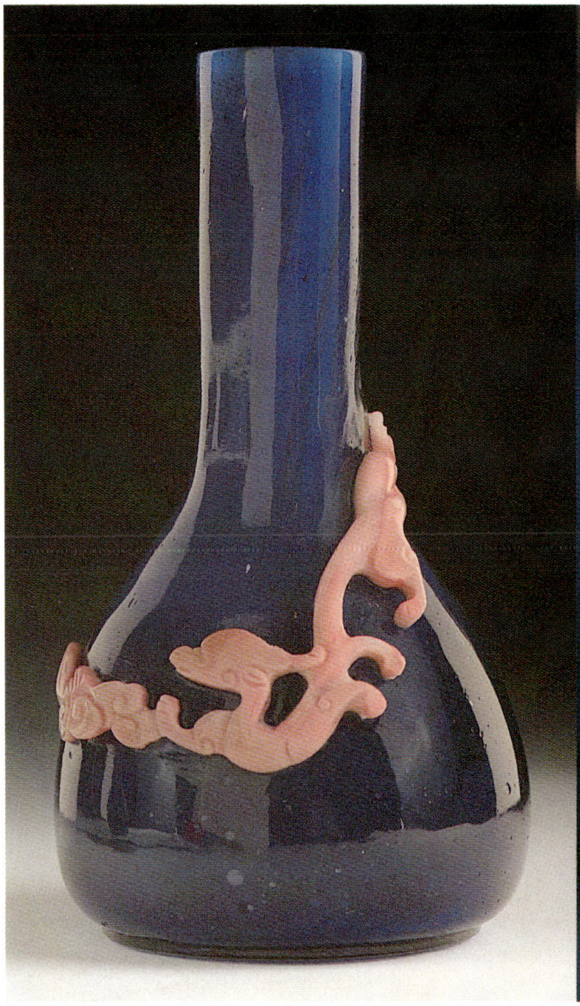

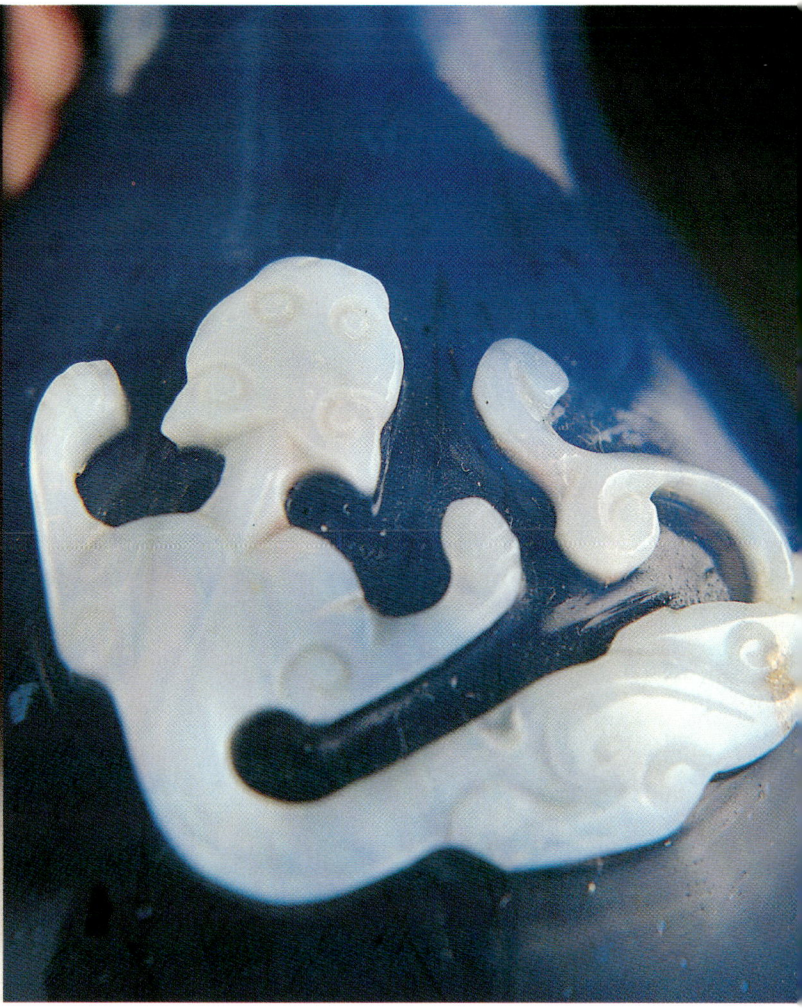

53

Vase

Transparent blue glass with partial inner casing of opaque white and carved overlays of opaque pink and white
Qing dynasty, 18 th century
H: 15,5 cm

The fairly thin walls of this mallet-shape vase turn slightly inward at the shoulder and ascend to a long, nearly cylindrical neck. The body is formed from a transparent blue glass. The entire neck has an additional inner casing of white glass which gives it a more opaque and solid appearance. Overlays of opaque pink on one main side and opaque white on the opposite side were individually applied to the ground and finely carved to represent two **zhilong** and small clouds. The body is supported on an unusually short foot ring that surrounds a deeply recessed base.

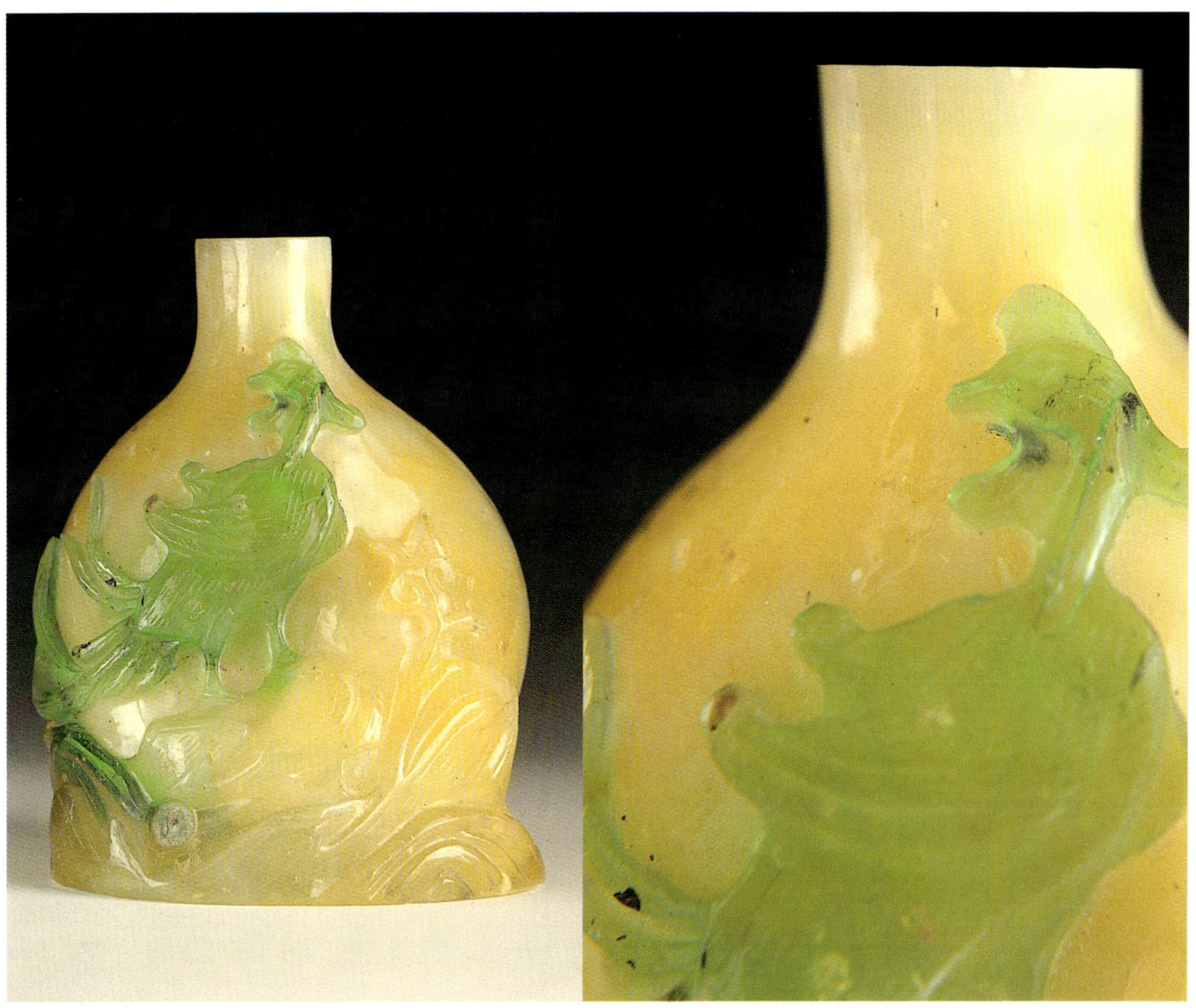

54

Jar supported on a rock work base

Translucent swirled yellow glass with carved overlays of transparent yellow, green and red
Qing dynasty, 18 th century
H: 10,2 cm

This **unusual, small vase** has a slightly asymmetrical spherical body from which rises a fairly short, nearly cylindrical neck. The body is formed from a transparent yellow and opaque white swirled glass. Overlays of transparent pale green, red and yellow have been individually applied to the ground. The pale green overlay is carved to represent a phoenix on one main side and the red overlay is carved to represent two clouds on the opposite side. The vessel is supported on a high foot of oval shape that is formed from a large yellow overlay applied to the body and naturalistically carved as a rock work. The underside is carved with a relatively wide foot that surrounds a deeply recessed base and also partially extends the exterior rock work.

55

Vase

Translucent white glass with carved overlays of transparent pale green, blue, red and yellow brown
Qing dynasty, 18th century
H: 15.3 cm

This vase has a cylindrical body that gently tapers toward the base and a broad cylindrical neck which flares slightly toward the top. The body is formed from a translucent white glass. Overlays of transparent pale green, blue, red and yellow- brown, all occasionally streaked with brown, have been individually applied and finely carved to represent lotus blossoms, leaves and a band of waves. The neck features several details carved from the blue overlay color including a wide rim incised with a squared spiral, a row of bosses below the rim as well as small sculptural **zhilong** which are exquisitely carved and applied to the narrow edges. The body is supported on a relatively high foot ring carved from the blue overlay color. The base is deeply recessed.

A glass snuff bottle in the collection of Mary and George Bloch is cased with overlay colors of identical transparent blue and transparent pale green streaked with brown as those which dominate in the present vase (see *Robert W. L. Kleiner*, ***Chinese Snuff Bottles from the Collection of Mary and George Bloch***, *Hong Kong, Herald International, 1987, page 78, n° 107*). The two overlay colors on the Bloch snuff bottle are also applied in a very similar arrangement as those on the present piece with the blue color overlay on the lower portion of the body and the green color overlay above it.

What makes the Bloch snuff bottle especially interesting is that both overlay'colors are retained in their original uncarved state thus giving us a general idea of the appearance of this vase before it was carved cameo style with its present design.

Special mention should be made of the **zhilong** that form the "handle" on each narrow side of the neck as both are exquisitely modeled and, in spite of their small size, have carefully carved features such as eyes, ears and a bifurcated tail. These two **zhilong** may be small in size, but they contribute greatly to the esthetic quality of the vase.

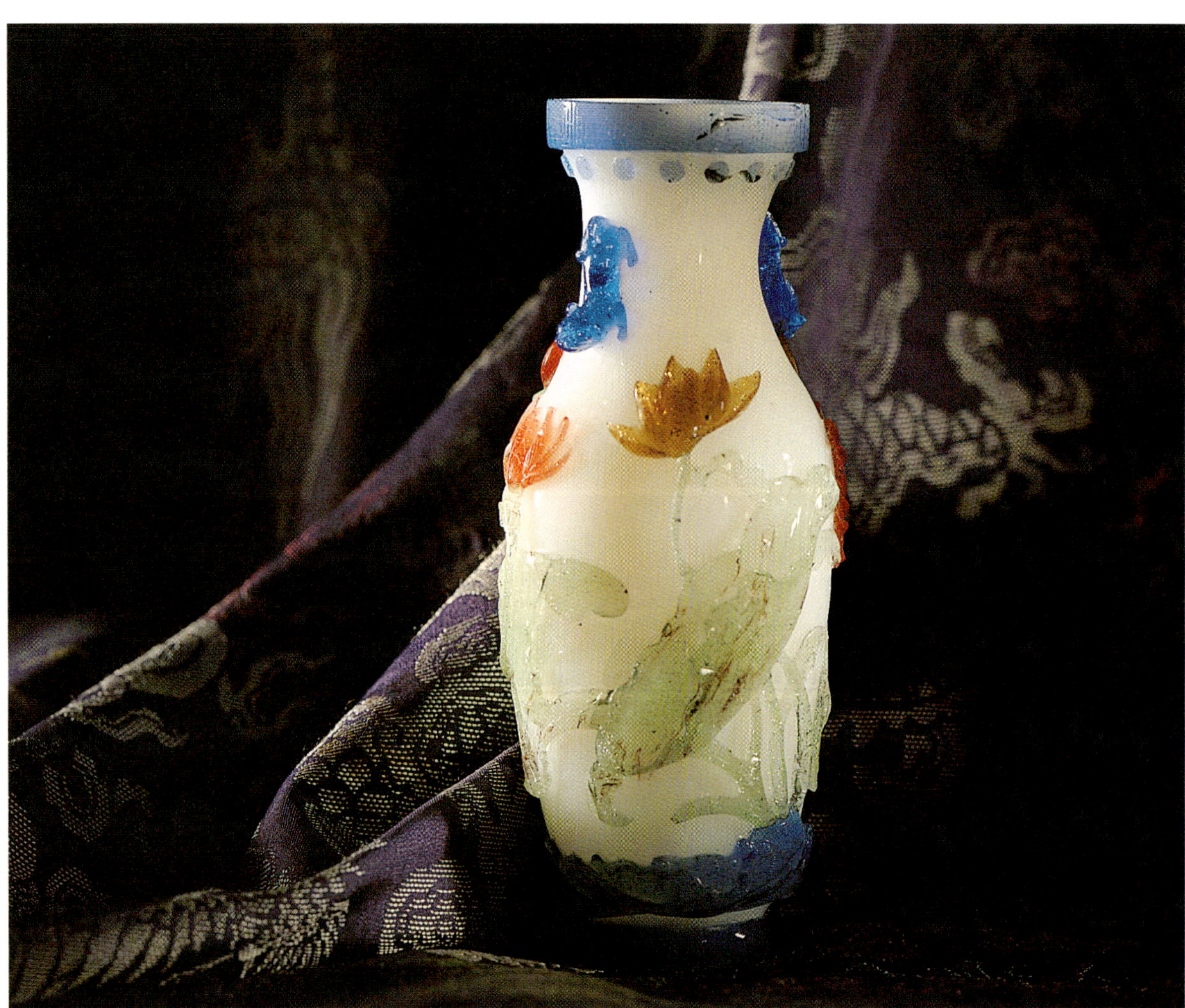

56

Vase of *gu* shape

Translucent pale blue glass with carved superimposed overlay of green over red
Qing dynasty, 19 th century
H: 15,5 cm

The body of this elegant *gu*-shape vase is formed from a thin, translucent blue glass with a slight opalescence. The ground has been entirely cased with transparent red over which a second dark green has been applied. The superimposed overlay is finely carved cameo style to represent a single prunus tree with numerous branches. The neck is widely flared and formed from slightly thinner and more transparent glass than the body. The neck has a thin rim carved from the overlays, though only the top layer of dark green color is visible. The foot is extremely short, matching the size of the rim on the neck, and is carved from the overlays with evidence of both layers. The base is slightly recessed.

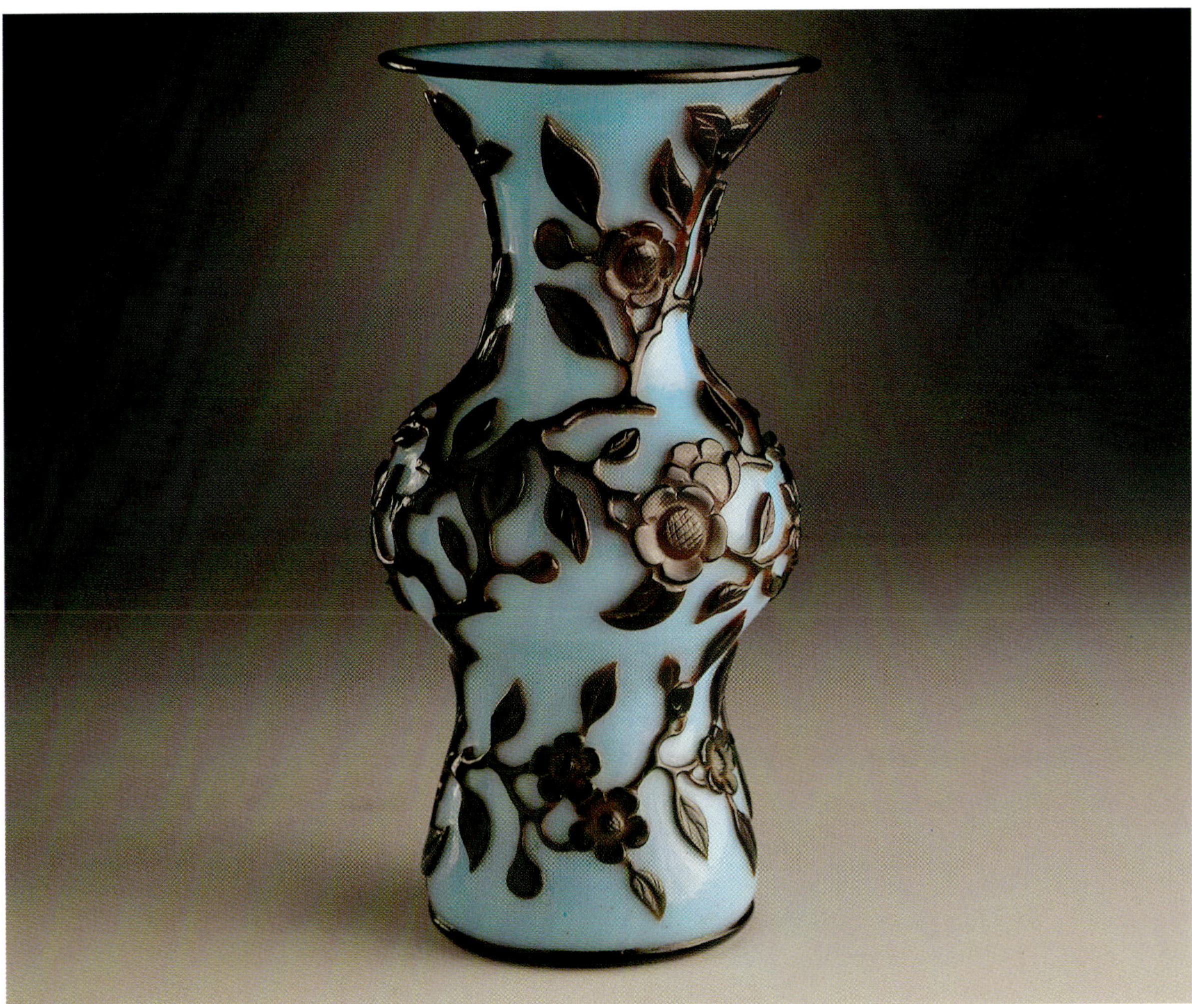

57

Vase

Opaque white glass with carved superimposed overlay of green over pink
Qing dynasty, 19 th century
H: 25,4 cm

This vase has a compressed globular body from which rises the extremely long, nearly cylindrical neck. The body is formed from an opaque white glass cased with opaque pink over which a second dark green has been applied. The superimposed overlay is carved cameo style to represent several squirrels wandering among fruiting grape vines. The neck of this vase is emphasized by the relatively large amount of pink color overlay that it retains and also by the wide rim carved from both overlays, though only the top layer of dark green color is visible on the exterior. The high foot ring is carved from the white ground, but retains traces of the overlay in the form of a wide band on the upper and lower edge. The base is deeply recessed.

The subject of squirrels among grapes was a common decorative motif in the Ming and Qing periods and is often found on porcelains and various kinds of carving. In the latter period it was an especially popular motif on snuff bottles (see, for example, the porcelain snuff bottle in the form of a crouching squirrel holding a cluster of grapes in Pamela R. Lessing Friedman, ***Chinese Snuff Bottles from the Pamela R. Lessing Friedman Collection****, exhibition catalogue, Hong Kong, Techpearl Printing, Ltd., 1990, page 151, cat. n° 126*).

This motif was the subject of an article by Ka Bo Tsang in which she convincingly argues that it is symbolic of fertility see, Ka Bo Tsang, “The 'Squirrel and Grape' Motif - Its Significance Reinterpreted” in the ***Journal of the International Chinese Snuff Bottle Society****, 1995, volume XXVII, n° 3, pages 15-19.*

A pair of vases cased with a nearly identical dark green and pink superimposed overlay on an opaque white body, but carved with a bird and flower motif is in the collection of Alan E. Feen and illustrated in, Emily Byrne Curtis, "Qing Imperial Glass" in Robert Kleiner, ***Chinese Snuff Bottles in the Collection of Mary and George Bloch****, British Museum Press, 1995, page XXVI, figure 10.*

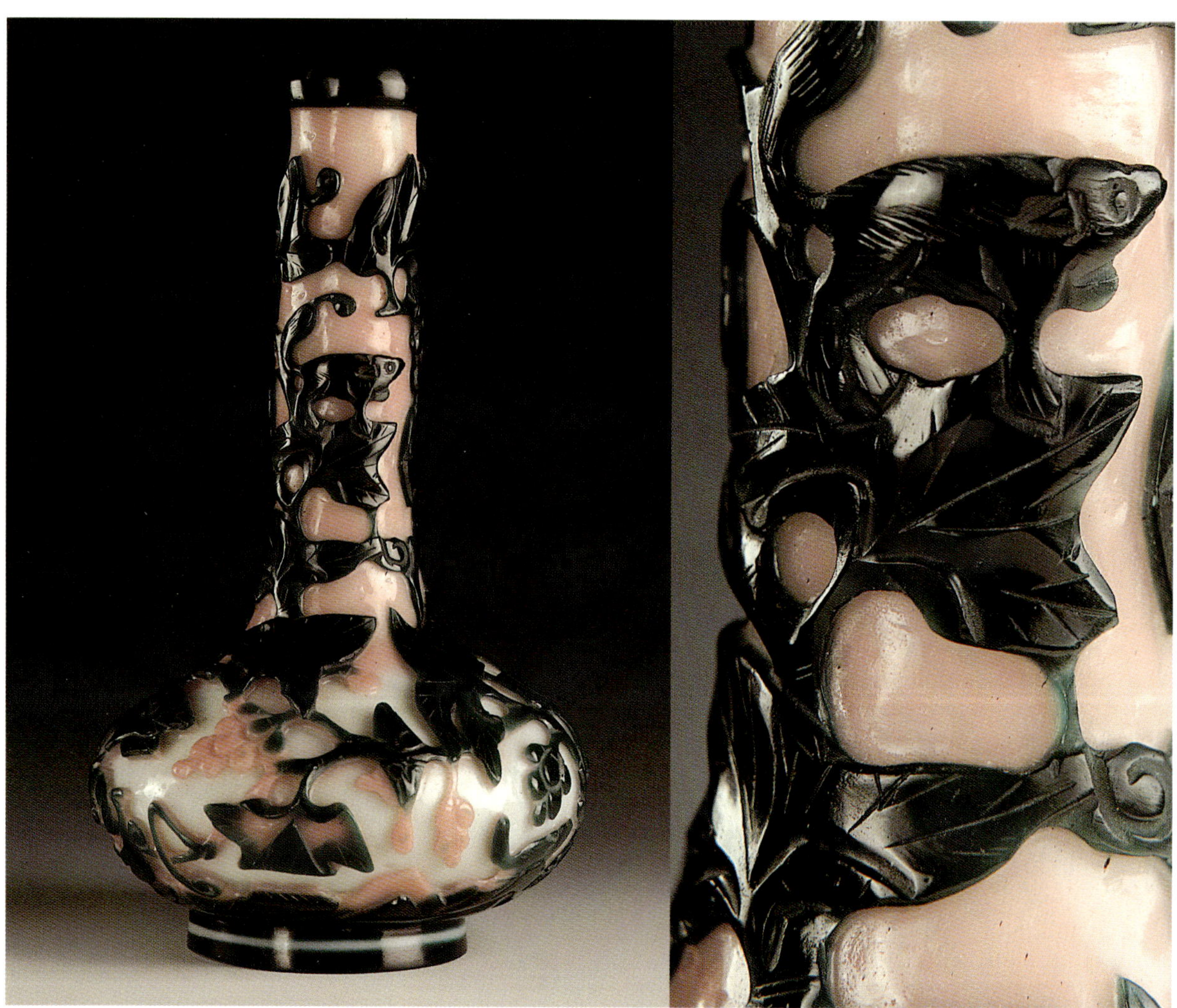

58

Figure of Li Bai

Opaque red-brown glass with gold flecks imitating aventurine
Qing dynasty, 18 th century
H: 9,3 cm

This small figure is boldly carved to represent the Tang poet Li Bai seated in a casual pose and holding a cup in one hand. The figure is carved from an opaque red-brown glass suffused with tiny gold flecks imitating aventurine. The glass has some thin striations that are of slightly darker tone as well as more transparent and do not include any gold flecks. It is interesting to note that the piece of glass from which this figure is carved is not very wide, especially if one considers that it is a sculptural piece. The narrowness of the glass used, however, is only truly obvious when the figure is viewed in profile. The base is flat and conforms to the shape of the lower edge on the exterior.

Aventurine glass, also called golden star glass, deserves much more attention and study than it has received in the recent past. Aventurine glass appears to have been introduced at a fairly early date in the Qing dynasty to China from Europe and it is uncertain when objects fashioned from aventurine glass began to be made from locally produced material rather than from imported one. Palace documents record that in 1741 two Jesuit missionaries working at the imperial glass workshop, Pierre d'Incarville and Gabriel-Leonard de Broussard, produced aventurine glass and translucent blue glass (see Yang Boda, "A Brief Account of Qing Dynasty Glass" in *Claudia Brown and Donald Rabiner*, ***Chinese Glass of the Qing Dynasty, 1644-1911: The Robert H. Clague Collection***, *exhibition catalogue, Phoenix Museum of Art, 1987, page 78*). It is, however, unfortunately not clear whether this refers to the production of two separate types of glass, aventurine glass and translucent glass, or to the combination of the two (possibly then still using imported material) such as is illustrated by the vase in the collection of Alan E. Feen in *Clarence Shangraw and Claudia Brown*, ***A Chorus of Colors: Chinese Glass from Three American Collections***, *exhibition catalogue, Asian Art Museum of San Francisco, 1995, page 64, cat. n° 36.*

The most common article produced in aventurine glass is snuff bottles (see, ***Masterpieces of Snuff Bottles in the Palace Museum***, *Beijing, Forbidden City Publishing House, The Woods Publishing Co., 1985, page 86, n° 67 and page 87, n° 68* for two examples from the Qianlong period). Figures carved from this glass material are relatively scarce and the thinness of the present figure illustrates the precious quality of this type of glass. A related figure of a seated Guanyin carved from aventurine glass, dated to the nineteenth century but also most likely of the eighteenth century date is illustrated in The Oriental Art Gallery, **Oriental Works of Art**, *London, 1992, n° 49.*

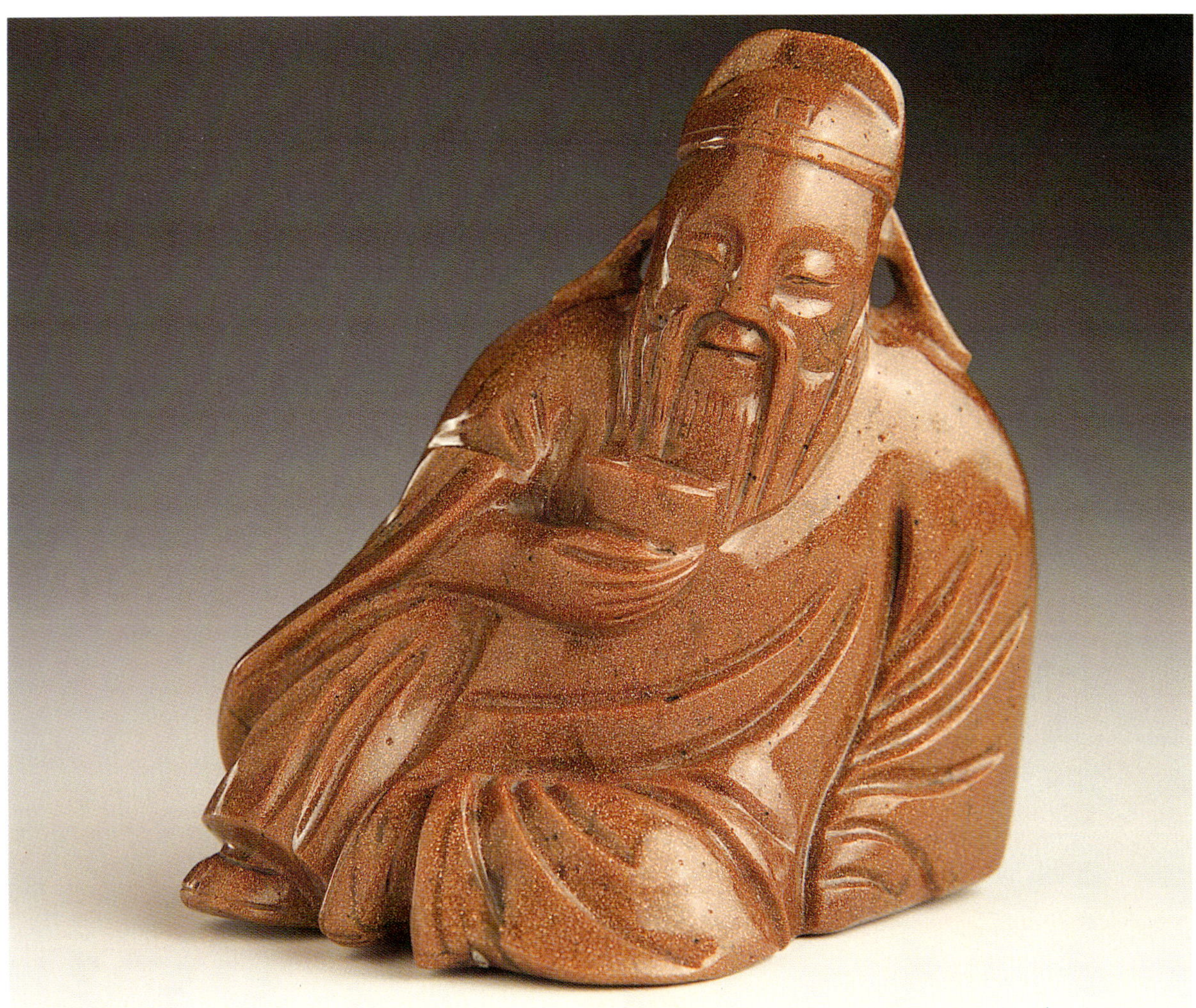

59

Figure of Guanyin

Transparent golden-brown glass imitating amber
Qing dynasty, 18th - early 19 th century
H: 11,2 cm

This small figure is carved to represent the bodhisattva Guanyin seated on rock work and holding a whisk in one hand and a vase in the other. The figure is carved from a transparent yellow-brown glass imitating amber. The flat base conforms to the shape of the lower edge on the exterior. The base is carved with a shallowy recessed horizontal band that suggests the edge of the exterior rock work and also depicts the underside of the figure's feet.

For a nearly identical, and possibly the same, figure, see Spink and Son, Ltd., ***Chinese Jewellery, Accessories and Glass***, *London, 1991, page 69, n° 116*.

Palace archives record that during the Yongzheng period amber (glass) cups with carved decoration were manufactured at the imperial palace glass workshop located in the Yuanming Yuan summer palace (see Yang Boda, "A Brief Account of Qing Dynasty Glass", in Brown and Rabiner, ***Chinese Glass of the Qing Dynasty, 1644-1911: The Robert H. Clague Collection***, *exhibition catalogue, Phoenix Art Museum, 1987, page 78*).

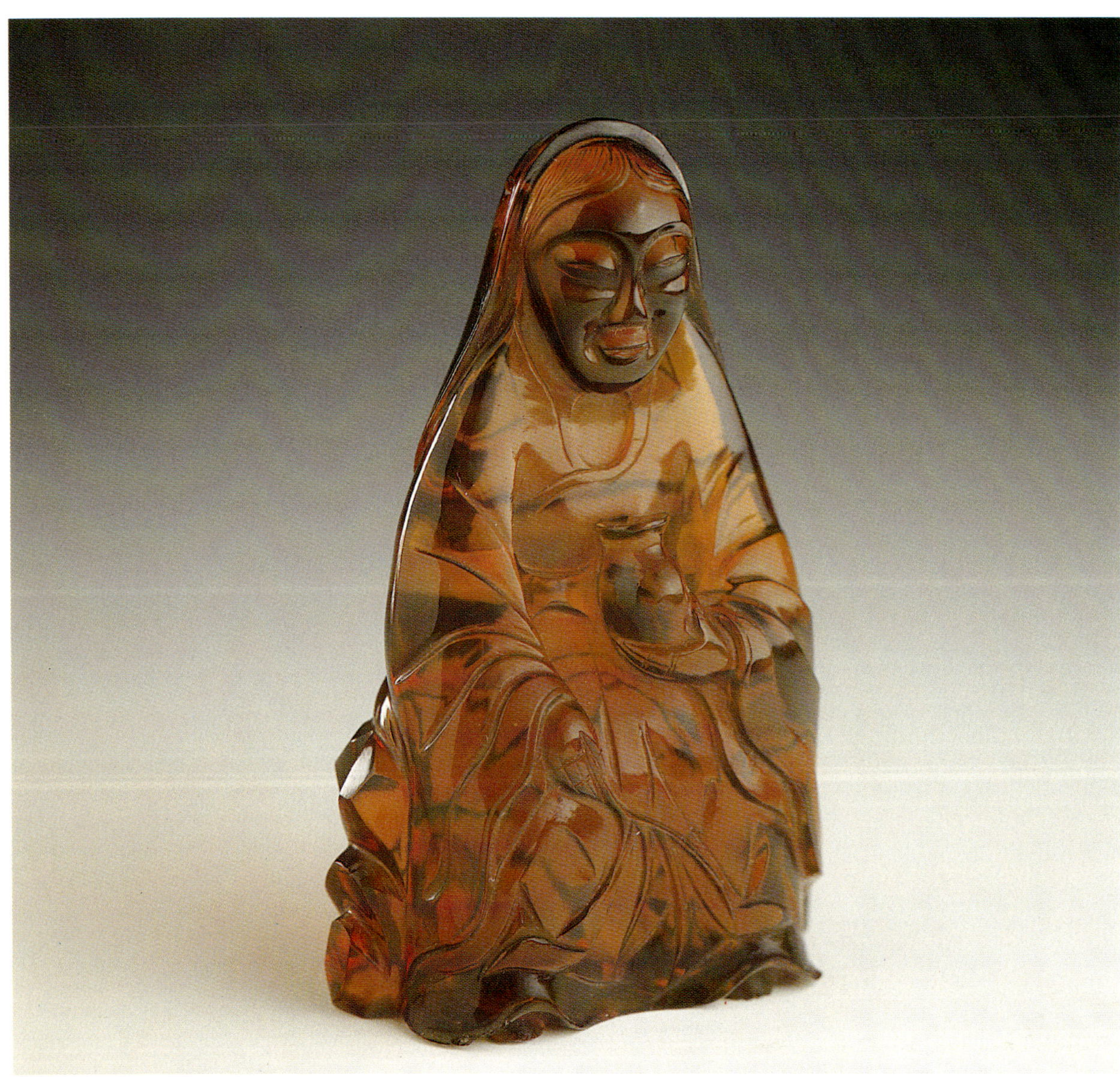

Figure of Guanyin

Opaque white glass imitating nephrite
Qing dynasty, 19 th century
H: 26,6 cm

This large standing figure of the bodhisattva Guanyin was fashioned by molding rather than by carving. Traces of the mold are still evident in the form of a thin unpolished vertical join on both the narrow sides. The figure is supported on a relatively short foot slightly smaller than the lower edge of the figure's costume and conforms to its shape. The base is flat. The glass is of opaque white color with some thin striations of slightly darker tones and imitates nephrite.

Molded figures representing Guanyin were produced in fairly large number and in an assortment of glass colors the majority of which appear to be made in imitation of other materials. In addition to the present figure of white glass imitating nephrite and the following example (*cat. n° 61*) of swirled green glass imitating jadeite several others have been published including one of transparent blue glass probably imitating lapis lazuli now in the Collection of the Hong Kong Museum of Art and illustrated in Brown and Rabiner, **Chinese Glass of the Qing Dynasty, 1644-1911: The Robert H. Clague Collection**, *exhibition catalogue, Phoenix Art Museum, 1987, page 48 n° 52* and another of transparent brown glass probably imitating amber in the Collection of the British Museum, London and illustrated in Harold Newman, **An Illustrated Dictionary of Glass**, *London, 1977, page 175.*

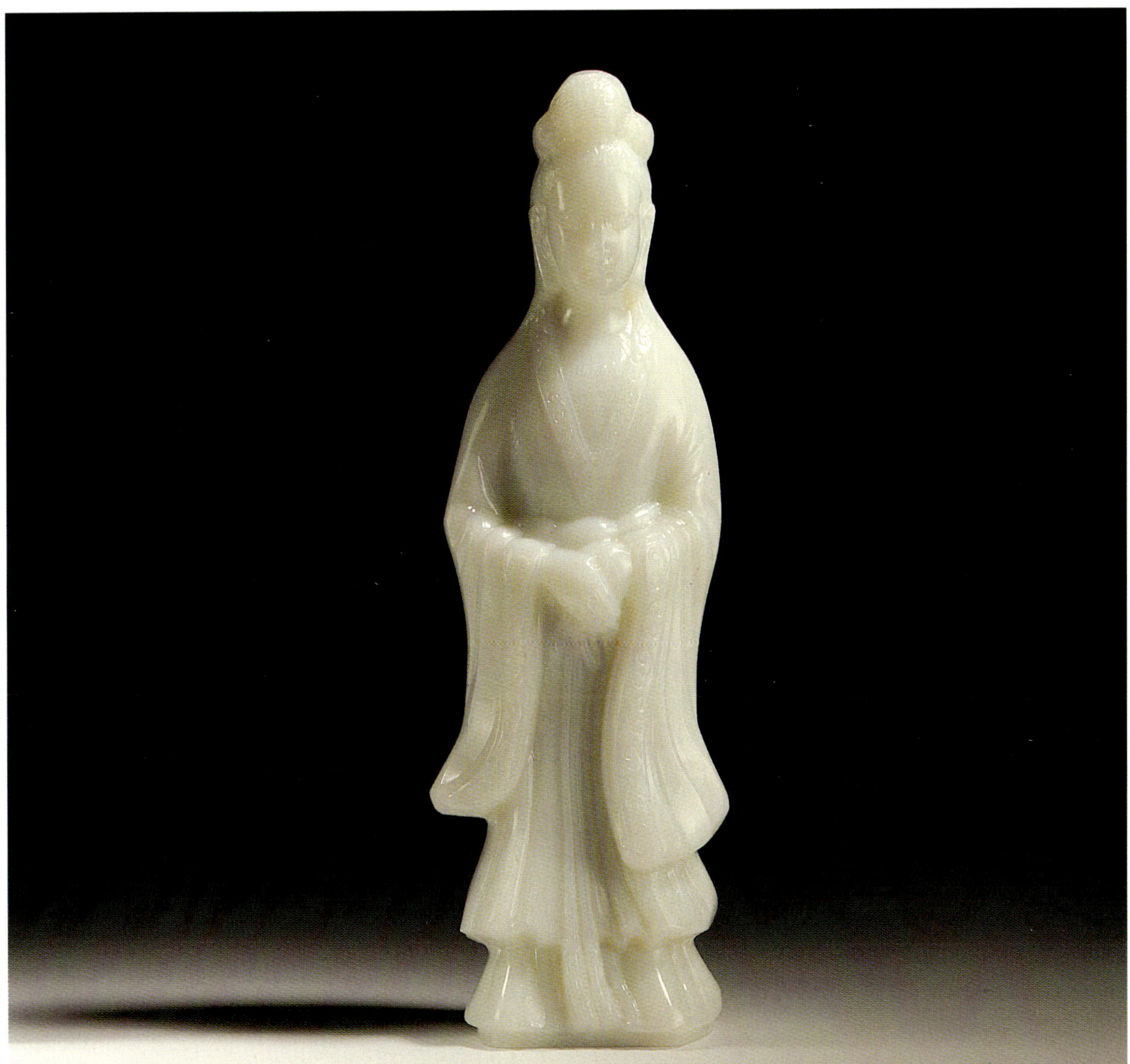

61

Figure of Guanyin

Striated opaque green glass imitating jadeite
Qing dynasty, 19 th century
H: 26,6 cm

This standing figure of the bodhisattva Guanyin is virtually identical, even in its dimensions, to the previous example (*n° 60*) and is possibly from the same mold. The only significant difference is that this example is formed from an opaque white and transparent green swirled glass that imitates jadeite. The flat base has been drilled later.

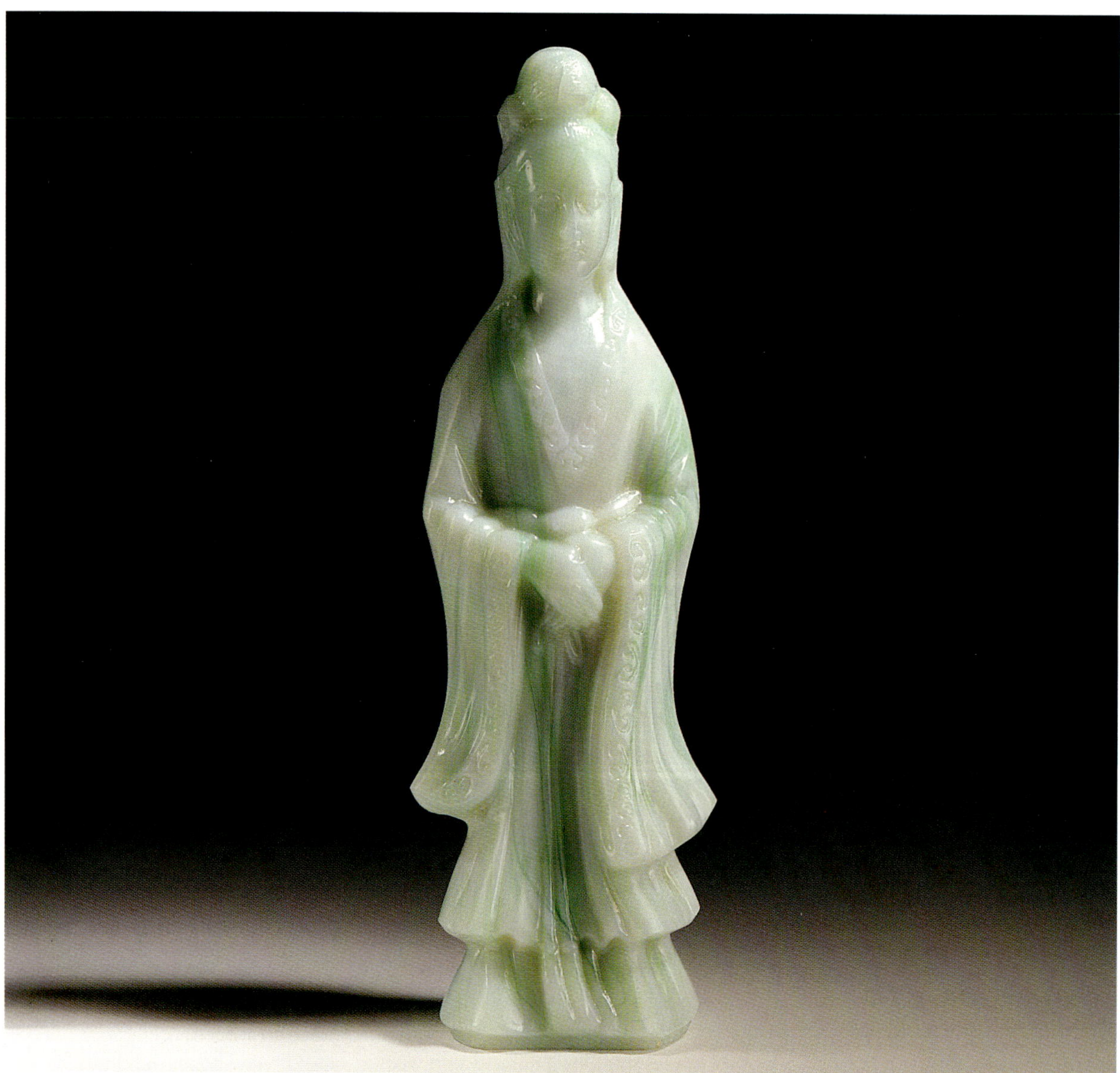

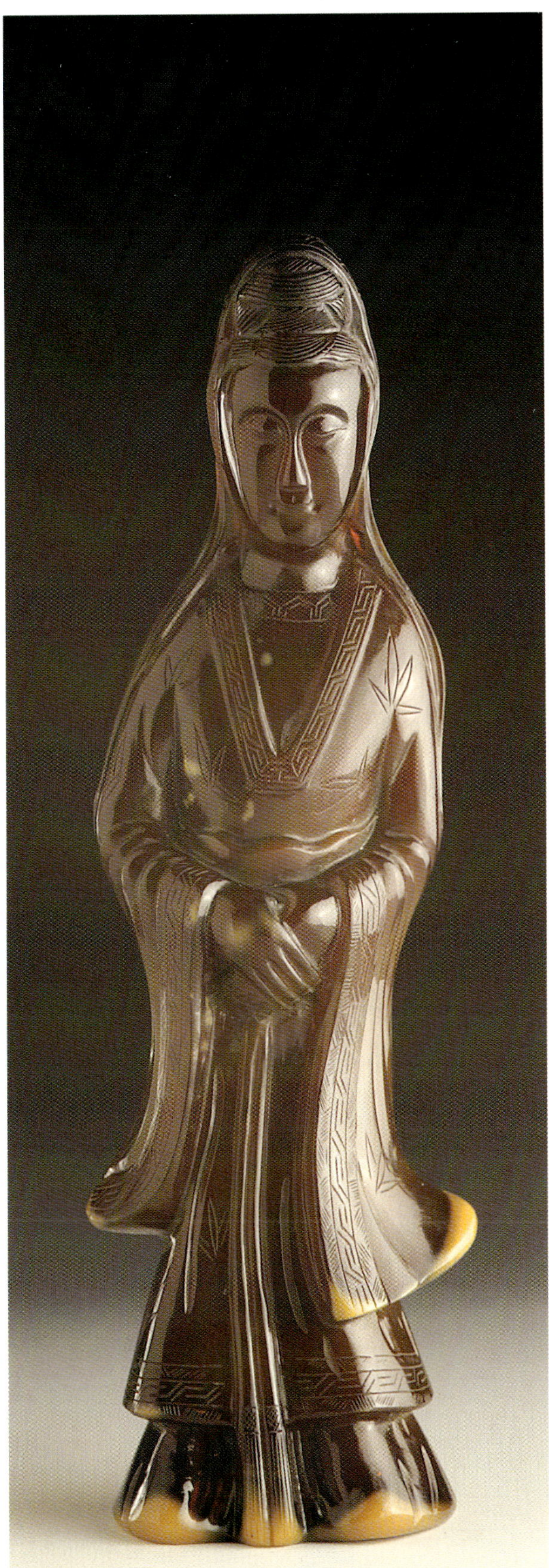

62

Figure of Guanyin

Transparent brown glass swirled with opaque yellow-brown imitating amber
Qing dynasty, 18 th - 19 th century
H: 26,4 cm

This **lovely standing figure** of the bodhisattva Guanyin was fashioned by molding rather than by carving. The vertical join left by the mold on both the narrow sides have been smoothly finished. This molded figure, unlike the previous two examples, includes incised details such as the bamboo pattern and geometric border that decorate the robe and the thin strands of the Guanyin's hair. These finely incised details greatly enhance the appearance and sculptural quality of the figure and also give it an individual personality. The base is flat and conforms to the shape of the lower edge of the exterior. The glass is of transparent brown color swirled with an opaque yellow brown. This yellow-brown color has been sensitively used to emphasize the edge of one sleeve and the lower edge of the costume and tassels.

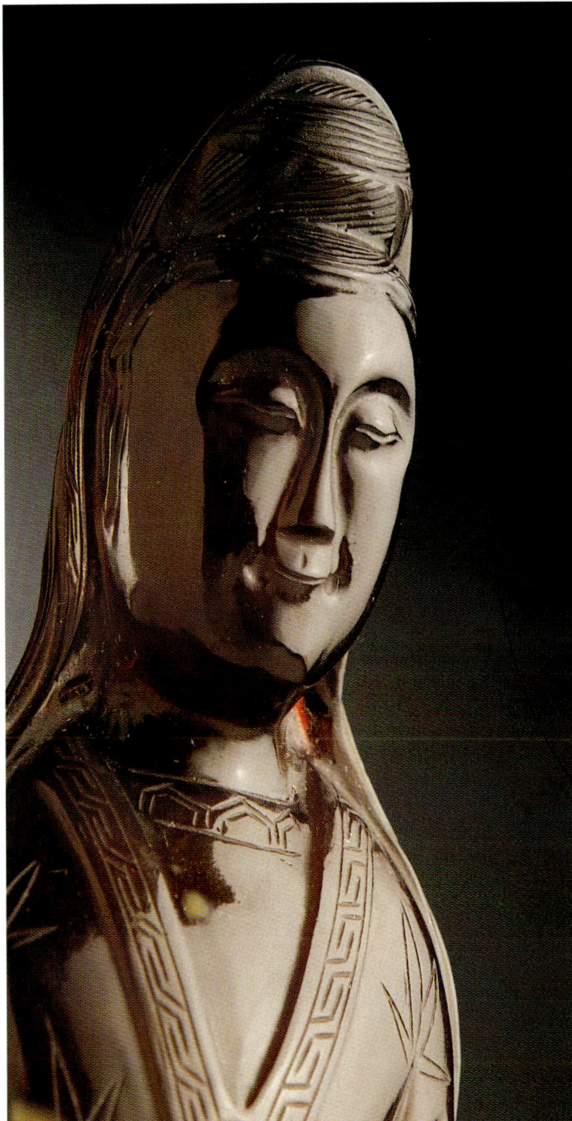

Selected Bibliography

- **Ayers, John.** *"Chinese Glass" in The Arts of the Ch'ing Dynasty*, exhibition catalogue, London: The Arts Council of Great Britain and the Oriental Ceramics Society, 1964.
- **Blount, Berniece and Henry**, *French cameo Glass*, Wallace-Homestead Company, Des Moines, Iowa, 1968.
- **Brill, Robert H. and Martin, John H.**, *Scientific Research in Early Chinese Glass*, Corning, New York: The Corning Museum of Glass, 1991.
- **Brown, Claudia and Rabiner, Donald**, *Clear as Crystal, Red as Flame: Later Chinese Glass*, exhibition catalogue, New York: China House Gallery, China Institute of America, 1990.
- **Brown, Claudia and Rabiner, Donald**, *Chinese Glass of the Qing Dynasty, 1644-1911*, The Robert H. Clague Collection, exhibition catalogue, Phoenix Art Museum, 1987.
- **Charleston, Robert J.**, *Masterpieces of glass: A World of History from the Corning Museum of Glass*, New York, 1980.
- **Curtis, Emily Byrne**, *"Qing Imperial Glass" in Kleiner, Robert, Chinese Snuff Bottles in the Collection of Mary and George Bloch*, British Museum Press, 1995.
- **Geng Baochang and Zhao Binghua**, *Zhongguo biyanhu zenschang*, Hong Kong, Joint Publishing and Taikong Culture Enterprise, 1992.
- **Donnelly, P. J.**, *Blanc de Chine*, Faber and Faber, London, 1969.
- **Dohrenwend, Doris**, *Glass in China: A Review Based on the Collection of the Royal Ontario Museum,* Oriental Art 26 (1980-1981), 422-46.
- **Gabbert, Gunhild**, *Chinesisches Glas*, exhibition catalog, Frankfurt-am-Main, Museum für Kunsthandwerk, 1980.
- **Honey, William B.**, *Chinese Glass*, Transactions of the Oriental Ceramics Society 17 (1939-40), 35-47.
- **Ka Bo Tsang**, *"The 'Squirrel and Grape' Motif - Its Significance Reinterpreted"*, in the *Journal of the International Chinese Snuff bottle Society*, 1995, Volume XXVII, n° 3.
- *Kangxi, Yongzheng, Qianlong Qing Porcelain from the Palace Museum Collection, Beijing*, Forbidden City Publishing House, The Woods Publishing Co., 1989.
- **Kleiner, Robert, Yang Boda and Shangraw, Clarence**, *Chinese Snuff Bottles: A Miniature Art from the Collection of Mary and George Bloch*, exhibition catalogue, Hong Kong Museum of Art, 1994.
- **Kleiner, Robert,** *Chinese Snuff Bottles in the Collection of Mary and George Bloch*, British Museum Press, 1995.
- **Lessing Friedman, Pamela R.**, *Chinese Snuff Bottles from the Pamela R. Lessing Friedman Collection*, exhibition catalogue, Hong Kong, Techpearl Printing, Ltd., 1990.

- **Lynn, Richard John,** Trans, *"Researches done during spare time into the realm of yong Lu God of the nose. The Yonglu xianjie of zhad zhigian"*, in the journal of the international chinese Snuff Bottle Society, 1991, vol XIII, n°3.
- *Masterpieces of Snuff Bottles in the Palace Museum,* Beijing, forbidden City Publishing House, the woods Publishing Co, 1985.
- **Mowry, Robert D.**, *Hare's Fur, Tortoiseshell and Partridge Feathers: Chinese Brown- and Black- Glazed Ceramics, 400-1400*, Harvard University Art Museum, 1996.
- **Newman, Harold**, *An Illustrated Dictionary of Glass*, London, 1977.
- **Phelps, Warren**, *"Later Chinese Glass, 1650-1900", in Journal of Glass Studies*, volume 19 (1977), 84-126.
- **Plesch, Peter H.**, *"Some Decorative Techniques Found in Later Chinese Glass",* Transactions of the Oriental Ceramics Society 44 (1979-80) 47-66.
- **Plesch, Peter H.**, *Some Approaches to the Study of Later Chinese Glass,* in *Festschrift für Peter Wilhelm Meister*, Hamburg, Annaliese Ohm und Horst Reber, 1975.
- **Shangraw, Clarence**, *"Reflections on the Qing Imperial glasshouse (1696-1911) in A Miniature Art from the Collection of Mary and George Bloch*, exhibition catalogue, Hong Kong Museum of Art, 1994.
- **Shangraw, Clarence and Brown, Claudia**, *A Chorus of Colors: Chinese Glass from Three American Collections*, exhibition catalogue, Asian Art Museum of San Francisco, 1995.
- **Sotheby Parke Bernet and Co.**, *A Collection of Chinese Pekin Glass,* The Property of Professor P. H. and Mrs. T. Plesch, London, November 12, 1979.
- **Spink and Son, Ltd.**, *Chinese Jewellery, Accessories and Glass*, London, 1991.
- **Tian Jiaqing**, *"Early Qing furniture in a set of Qing Dynasty Court Painting"*, in Orientations, january 1993, volume 24, n°1.
- *Tributes from Guangdong to the Qing Court*, exhibition catalogue, jointly presented by the Palace Museum, Beijing and the Art Gallery, The Chinese University of Hong Kong, 1987
- **Watt, James C. Y.**, *Chinese Jades from Han to Ch'ing*, exhibition catalogue, The Asia Society, New York, 1980.
- **Woodward, Hiram W., Jr.**, *Asian Art in the Walters Art Gallery: a Selection*, Baltimore, 1991.
- **Yang Boda**, *"A Brief Account of Qing Dynasty Glass" in Brown, Claudia and Rabiner, Donald, Chinese Glass of the Qing Dynasty, 1644-1911:* The Robert H. Clague Collection, exhibition catalogue, Phoenix Art Museum, 1978.

Lec.
édition

24, rue Feydeau. 75002 Paris. France
Tel : (33) 01 40 13 78 13 Fax : (33) 01 40 13 78 18